ng this

NEWS INFORMATION

NEWS INFORMATION

The Organisation of Press Cuttings in the Libraries of Newspapers and Broadcasting Services

GEOFFREY WHATMORE

(International Publishing Corporation)

ARCHON BOOKS

HAMDEN, CONNECTICUT : 1965

First published 1964 by
Crosby Lockwood & Son Limited
26 Old Brompton Road, London, SW7

Published in the U.S.A by
Archon Books. The Shoe String Press Inc.

---

*Made and printed in Great Britain by
Richard Clay (The Chaucer Press), Ltd.,
Bungay, Suffolk*

Acknowledgements

It's usual to say, in the hackneyed phrase, that without the help of various people this book could not have been written. That would not be quite true in the present case but undoubtedly it has benefited enormously from the freely given time of a large number of librarians who have shown their libraries to me and collectively spent many hours demonstrating their techniques and special systems.

Among them I would mention first Mr Roworth Lintott, Librarian of the *Daily Mirror*, a library at the heart of the largest group of publishing companies in the world, serving a newspaper with sales in excess of five million copies a day. In the course of a series of conversations matching my experience in the library of a small class newspaper, with his knowledge of the requirements of a popular daily, we have together become more clear on a number of fundamental points of principle and he has provided a wealth of practical examples.

I would like to express my thanks also to Mr J. Lonsdale, Head of *The Times* Intelligence Department, who planned the newest and the best laid out library in Fleet Street from its beginnings. I make no apologies for quoting over and again examples of the practice of both these libraries because they seem to me to offer, more than most, signposts to the way ahead for news libraries.

I am greatly indebted also to Mr Lawrence Ardern, Librarian of the Scottish College of Commerce, Mr Donald Pigott, Librarian of the Associated Octel Company, Bletchley Laboratory, and Mr Frank Singleton, Librarian of *The Guardian*, Manchester, all of whom have devoted much time to reading the manuscript, and who have made valuable suggestions.

In the course of my investigations I met also Miss E. Campbell, Press Librarian of the Royal Institute of International Affairs,

Mr Roger Curtis, Head of the B.B.C. News Libraries, Mr E. A. Harwood, Librarian of the *Daily Telegraph*, Mr Ben Howell, Librarian of the Press Association, Mr A. E. Kuhnberg, Librarian of the *Financial Times*, Miss C. B. O'Grady, Librarian of the Reuter Library, Mr Stanley Pryor, Librarian of Associated Newspapers, and Mrs I. Wagner, Librarian of the Labour Party Library, who between them sparked off many ideas—and some disagreements—which have influenced the text of this book.

By no means least important is the help I have received from friends across the Atlantic. In particular from Mr Joe Molloy, the peripatetic Librarian of the *Philadelphia Inquirer*, who not only provided me with comment and samples from his own library stationery and some excellent pictorial material, but took the opportunity to canvas on my behalf his colleagues at the Special Libraries Association Newspaper Division St Louis Convention of 1964.

Contents

List of Plates

(between pages 86 and 87)

CHAPTER ONE

Why Press Cuttings?

In this rapidly changing world few things get out of date so quickly as information. On almost any subject except perhaps historical ones situations change faster than books can be written or published. As a result, books alone are not nowadays sufficient in themselves as sources of reference, and if up-to-date information is required they must be supplemented by other material. So we see in libraries, particularly those carrying out a specialist function, an ever increasing emphasis on non-book materials—periodicals, official documents, scientific reports—as sources of information.

This is especially true of organizations concerned with current affairs, a subject which by its nature is constantly developing and changing. In this field, books fall into the background as research sources and the bulk of the information can only be supplied by reference to newspapers. The resources of newspapers, however, are so vast that the sheer scale of the task of making their contents available for retrospective reference seems to have overawed those who might wish to make use of them in this way.

Quite apart from broadcast news, nearly 100 million copies of national daily newspapers are distributed in Britain every week—and this takes no account of Sunday papers and the provincial press. The volume of information they contain is virtually limitless—and much of it is of great importance. It is there for the day, and then it is gone. Today's paper is followed by tomorrow's; yesterday's is quickly forgotten. The remarkable fact is that from the library and research point of view information from newspapers is very poorly organized. Yesterday's news—and last month's—is not only stale, it is largely inaccessible. For in spite of this enormous output of facts and figures—or perhaps because of it—it remains difficult and sometimes impossible to trace a news report of which the date is imperfectly known. The trend of events on some much discussed topic of the day is likewise often difficult to refer to in retrospect.

There are, in fact, only two British published sources of reference to the general contents of the press which are widely used. These are *The Times Index*, which is published in volumes covering two months at a time, and *Keesing's Contemporary Archives*, a digest from the world's newspapers published weekly with cumulative indexes. The Library Association's *British Humanities Index*, mainly concerned with periodicals, includes additionally some of the feature articles from *The Guardian* and *The Times*. *The Glasgow Herald* publishes its own index. There is also a small number of published indexes and abstracts of a specialized nature. But the overall coverage of the press by digests and indexes is inadequate for the scale of the output of news. As a result, the key dates are elusive.

Even when the date of a news item is known it is often difficult to refer to it. It is a great pity that it is still not easy to consult back numbers of any national newspapers other than *The Times* anywhere except the British Museum Newspaper Library in the suburbs of North London. This is the national collection of newspapers and includes also a number of foreign publications. Bound files of newspapers may be examined at the library but unbound copies cannot normally be consulted. A photocopying service is operated for the reproduction items of which the date is known. As far as it goes the library does a valuable job, but only a trickle of inquirers find their way to it and consultation by post is unsatisfactory.

Nothing remotely approaching this collection in size exists elsewhere in the United Kingdom. In Fleet Street, the facilities for consultation of their own back issues offered in many newspaper offices are far from ideal. Most public libraries retain *The Times* and perhaps the local provincial paper indefinitely, but little else except for short periods. The sale of back issues by the newspapers themselves varies from a few months in the case of *The Guardian* to several years for the *Financial Times* and *Daily Telegraph*. Photocopies are sometimes available for sale provided the date of the news item required can be traced.

This shortage of good reference facilities is the more surprising because current information is vital to us all since it directly affects our daily lives. There are a number of important subjects which are written about only in newspapers, or for which, at least, the newspaper is a major channel of communication. Newspapers are the main source for current reports and discussions on politics, foreign affairs, and social legislation, for instance. When reference is required to traffic regulations, new town planning proposals, speeches, election results, the work of the United Nations, trade in overseas territories, problems of national defence, all these vital matters in addition to the arts, sport, crime, entertainment, and many other topics of wide interest, a newspaper is the best starting point and often sufficient in itself.

Newspapers themselves, with the two exceptions referred to, do not regard it as part of their responsibility to provide for the public a key to their own past contents. Most of them do, however, maintain a comprehensive reference service for their own use—consisting in the main of classified collections of press cuttings.

The essential requirement is a library of the contents of the press, relating not only to yesterday's newspaper, but to the newspapers of five weeks, five months and, to less extent, of five years ago. Established newspapers have pioneered the way but, uncharacteristically, they have said little about it. How news library collections are best organized is the theme of this book.

Having perforce to set up libraries, partly as sources of information and partly as indexes to the contents of their own columns, newspapers began years ago by pragmatic methods to organize these accumulations of press cuttings entirely without regard to the work of librarians concerned with books or other materials. Very often, too, without regard to each other. Each newspaper, although only a stone's throw from the offices of its competitors in Fleet Street, has proceeded in its own way, shaping a system brick by brick, to build a service conditioned by the demands made on it.

The remarkable thing is, that while each newspaper library has developed isolated from others, they have all arrived at broadly the same solutions. Obviously, the methods in common must have a large measure of practical success to commend them. They are applicable not only to newspaper libraries, but to the libraries of broadcasting organizations and any other bodies requiring access to current information on a wide scale.

The methods employed have grown up under the tyranny of the clock and the manner of their use has conditioned their organization. A news library is subordinate to the larger organization which it serves and, more than most, its arrangement must to a considerable degree be tailored to the needs of its users.

An example of its use by a newspaper is the best way to illustrate the function of the library.

Suppose a burst reservoir causes major flooding and destruction in a small town. The event occurs on a Sunday afternoon. First news is flashed by Press Association tapes to the news desk and a reporter is sent straight from his home to the scene of the disaster. It is a long journey and by the time he gets there it only wants an hour or so to the last copy deadline for the first edition. The reporter has a quick look round, collects all the information he can in the time available, and dictates a story to his newspaper over long distance telephone. In the office the copy-taker takes down the text direct on to his typewriter, equipped with several carbons.

This is a big story, time is short, and the copy is rushed a sheet at a time to the sub-editorial department where it is prepared for the press. The reporter has given only the barest details. He has hazarded a guess at the population of the town. Is the figure correct? There is just time to send some of the copy to the library for checking, and out come the gazeteers and, perhaps, the last census figures. The dam was constructed about five years ago according to the story. Can the chief sub-editor have the cuttings on its opening? How much water does a ten-acre reservoir hold, anyway?

The story goes to press, and in the pause between that edition and the next the reporter on the spot comes through again. He has been told that a warning was given recently that the dam was unsafe. Was this reported at the time? Never mind, the library had turned up that item half an hour ago and the name of the local councillor concerned is passed on to the reporter for a follow-up interview.

Later, the editor thinks a list of similar previous occurrences would embellish the story and the library sets to work again. It is Sunday night and impossible to use any external source of reference, but if the library is lucky there may be a list already in existence, used on some previous occasion, perhaps by a rival newspaper.

Such a story may continue over several days and the library will be called upon by leader writers and the features staff for more background, more facts and figures about reservoirs and the construction of dams. When was the last debate in the House on water supplies? It is not unusual for several people to want the same material at the same time. Merely to reply that the file is out and first come first served will not do. So in some of the larger libraries a system has grown up of extensive duplication.

The foregoing example is treated at some length because it

illustrates the nature of the demand made on all news libraries from time to time. The library must be able to supply the latest information accurately and quickly. It must be as self-sufficient as possible since it is in use when alternative sources of reference are closed, and it will deal with a range of information, some of which is not to be found in books at all. Although the stock will consist overwhelmingly of press cuttings, it must not be exclusively so. It cannot do its job properly unless it maintains in addition an up-to-date collection of quick reference books and a large number of pamphlets, periodicals, government publications, and other special source material which go to make up the documentation of our times.

In most news libraries the general run of inquiries can be answered in two or three minutes, a great many are satisfied in one minute or less. To offer busy inquirers a number of books—or even marked passages—in answer to their questions is the wrong approach. It is the news librarian's job to provide information, not books, and to provide it in the simplest form, which is often a press cutting. The arrangement of the library must itself be simple in order that the classification will aid, and not impede, the hurried search for relevant material.

Individually, newspapers are cheap. We should not assume, however, that because a single newspaper only costs a few coppers, a press cuttings library is cheap to run. A subscription to *The Times* costs over £11 a year and a minimum of two copies are needed for cutting. Compare this charge with the annual cost of a copy of *Who's Who*, for example, or *Keesing's Contemporary Archives*. But there is incomparably more information in a year's issue of *The Times*, if properly organized. For the purposes of newspapers cutting mainly their own paper the supply of source material costs very little. For other types of organization, however, the cost of large numbers of newspapers daily can be deceptively high.

Much of the material filed in a news library is retained for a limited period only (a matter of months in some instances).

The maximum life of a press cutting, depending on the space available and the purpose of the collection, is seldom more than two decades or so. With most it is far less. A few Fleet Street collections, surprisingly, date from the beginning of the century and can still produce cuttings of that period. Here and there are hidden treasure troves like complete sequences of *Whitaker's Almanack* and *Wisden*, but these are exceptions.

Some classes of cuttings—such as those contributing to the local collection at a public library—are intended for permanent preservation as historical record. This book is not concerned with such items, which, of course, require quite different treatment. Generally speaking, bound files, microfilm, and books serve the long term needs of a news library, whose main concern is today and the recent past.

An important quality all news libraries must possess if they are to be successful is adaptability to change. Each must reflect the changing emphasis of the day's news. The questions asked of them are lively, human, and topical. Their arrangement is planned to a flexible system accommodating any number of new subjects and aspects of subjects. The staff rapidly acquire a wide (if skin deep) knowledge of current affairs and a phenomenal corporate memory. They take a pride, however—or should do—in finding by system and not by recollection.

Because many news libraries serve organizations concerned with mass communications in one way or another they are the natural recipients of quantities of ephemeral and largely unlisted material—press handouts, advertisement brochures, embassy bulletins and radio monitoring reports—all of which, if imaginatively organized, can be brought together with press cuttings and indexes to form a library of fascinating variety.

For a little time the day's news is preserved here in association according to the accident of the alphabet. Anarchists and assassinations, monarchy and mohammedanism, earthquakes, eclipses, the divorces of duchesses, the promises of politicians, are ranked side by side. The library must be able to provide the aphorisms of Ustinov, the terms of the last Russian note, the cost of Skybolt or list the husbands of Elizabeth Taylor, at a moment's notice.

A place of delight to browse in perhaps. But no place for sluggards. Few libraries are busier, and the required result is only achieved by tidy minds, disciplined organization, and a great deal of routine drudgery which is the basis of success.

CHAPTER TWO

Staff, Layout, Furniture and Equipment

(i) STAFF

A LIBRARY service that is used all round the clock, day and night, needs a large staff. It does not, however, require to be fully staffed the whole time. The library of a newspaper may provide a service from around nine in the morning until well after midnight. The heaviest demand comes in the late afternoon and early evening for morning newspapers (which are, of course, edited and printed at night) and between 8 a.m. and 4 p.m. for evening papers. Outside those times the library has a skeleton staff and there are opportunities for the early and late duty people to clear a good deal of essential routine.

Some examples of staffing may be of interest. The *Daily Mirror* employs 47 in its library with a maximum of 30 working at one time. From 11 p.m. till 4 a.m. only two persons are present. Since the staff works a five day week and the library, which also serves the *Sunday Mirror*, is in use every day, a shift system is essential.

The Press Association library has a staff of 13, open 23 hours a day. The *Financial Times* employs 14 people. The B.B.C. news library, doing a very similar job to the newspaper libraries, has twelve, although 62 more are employed in additional B.B.C. cuttings collections elsewhere.

Across the Atlantic the *New York Times* employs 89 in its libraries and information department (including the published index).

Many small news libraries manage effectively with only one person. The problems of the one-man library, however, are much simplified, for there are no difficulties over delegation. The man who recovers the information is also the one who originally filed it—which makes classification easier, or at least less vital. Organization and arrangement assume major importance again, however, if the collection is expected to be consulted in the librarian's absence. This is the hardest test of an efficient and clear filing system.

Clearly, a large library open day and night requires a librarian with a deputy capable of taking charge. The remainder of the staff is usually divided into markers, who mark and classify newspapers for cutting, and filing assistants who cut and file. A number may specialize in certain fields, like sport or biography.

Filing is a junior routine task, usually allocated to newcomers, but the success of the library depends on it being done accurately; some senior specialists, indeed, insist on doing their own filing. (Few libraries attempt to maintain rigid staff divisions, nor would it be desirable.) Ideally, the task of filing should be automatic, since the cuttings are marked with a symbol or key word indicating their destination.

Markers, who require a thorough acquaintance with the classification scheme, rely heavily on experience to ensure consistency and on foresight to anticipate the most useful placings. In order to classify properly it is essential to understand at least the elements of the subject being dealt with. The subject of a news library is the world, so some specialization of interest among the staff is worth encouraging.

In the library of a provincial newspaper, local affairs take the place of world affairs and familiarity with the locality, its history, and its personalities, is very necessary. Fortunately, under the pressure of the day's work, any alert person may rapidly gain such a store of general knowledge as to win a television quiz jackpot with ease. It has been done!

Many news libraries have not greatly changed or improved in the last 30 years. Nor are they likely to unless steps are taken to recruit the best human material, ideally with experience of the disciplines of libraries elsewhere.

What is not yet fully understood, by newspaper managements at any rate, is that the job of a news librarian requires education, training, and knowledge of certain principles. It is a skill that can be learned. The principles can be synthesized and taught. They are emphatically not best learned by the time-honoured method of 'sitting next to Nelly'.

It seems too often to be thought that a primary aptitude for the job is a flair for news. While undoubtedly useful, this is not of first importance. The basic need is understanding of the methods of organization of information, which are fundamentally the same whether the information is medical, aeronautical, or in the form of general news.

Until this vital question of staffing is given proper attention it is unlikely that news libraries can take full advantage of the magnificent source material available to them, nor can the library service itself be expected to reach full efficiency.

(ii) LAYOUT

Since the end of the last war a number of new news libraries have been established, chiefly by the television companies. Several long-established ones have been re-housed, among them the libraries of the *Daily Mirror*, the *Financial Times*, and *The Times*. It must be said with regret that even so few of them have sufficient space and furniture has often had to be cramped into an altogether inadequate area. The new Intelligence Department of *The Times* forms an admirable exception, where specially designed furniture lends an unusual air of spaciousness.

Like any other special library, a news library cannot exist on its own. It is part of the larger organization which it serves, and must compete for space with other departments. Consequently, it never has enough. Nor is it always correctly positioned in relation to its users. In most cases the librarian will be lucky if he is able to reveal his genius for planning other than through his powers of improvisation.

In a press or broadcasting organization the library is part of the editorial department, serving chiefly the editorial staff. It should be on the same floor as the other editorial sections, near enough to those who use it most to allow passage to and fro with minimum waste of time, yet situated so as to be aside from the commotion which sometimes affects editorial efforts. The *Daily Mirror* library provides a good example, placed between the *Daily Mirror* and *Sunday Mirror* editorial and next to the teleprinter room. It is important that users should not have to climb stairs to get to the library. Any department store chief will agree that the ground floor always does the best business. The new *Times* building again forms an exception here, where the Intelligence Department is reached by an open well staircase leading directly upward from the news room below.

The precise layout of the library will vary according to the shape of the space available and how many awkward corners are to be filled. It must be remembered also that it is not so much concerned with books as with larger, clumsier, and less compact newspapers. Provision has to be made for opening out newspapers for cutting, and for storage of loose newspaper files for reference.

Room should also be found, if it can possibly be spared, for overflow stocks. A basement room or an attic, even a room outside the building, provided it is warm and well ventilated, is an inestimable boon.

The space requirements and planning of the library depend first upon whether the whole of it is freely open to users or if inquirers are allowed no further than a counter, stating their needs to an assistant on duty there.

Obviously, if the library is open to all and users are encouraged to find what they want for themselves, some provision should ideally be made for reading desks and chairs, plenty of space between rows of filing cabinets and extensive guiding and labelling of drawers. If on-the-spot consultation is normal, with inquirers browsing in folders at the filing point, or quickly looking up a series of items for comparison, the library is going to need a good deal more space than a closed one. Such 'open access' tends to be discouraged by the larger libraries but elsewhere, if there is not sufficient staff to cope with several inquirers at once, an element of 'self service' inevitably grows up.

Undoubtedly the closed library is a much easier one to run. It can be planned more tightly with cabinets closer together. Where a counter keeps users at arms' length the librarian can control his stock more effectively, material does not so frequently go astray, and its issue and return can be recorded. Books stay in order on the shelves. Passage about the library is not impeded. In a word, it stays tidy. For the straightforward quick answering of most specific inquiries and for the issue of cuttings there is no doubt that the library runs more smoothly if it keeps its users at a distance from the filing cabinets. Any tidy-minded librarian wants to rule his domain in his own way, and self service is the enemy of good order.

It is doubtful, however, if the convenience of users should be subordinated to the needs of tidy organization. Indeed, in most special libraries it cannot be, for there are always those high-powered people who cannot be restricted to their own side of the counter. For certain kinds of inquiry, moreover, a general search by the inquirer himself has to be made, his idea of what he wants crystallizing as he pursues it.

It is obvious that the library must be well lit, well ventilated, and, if at all possible, have large windows and a good measure of natural light. Continuous preoccupation with newspaper reading is a strain on the eyes and the need for good lighting is rather greater than in an office. The ideal situation of a news library places it in a projecting wing of the building, not too far from its users, with windows on three sides. At the *Daily Telegraph* an interesting location places the library on a mezzanine floor, occupying three sides of an open square surrounding the entrance hall below.

In practice most news libraries consist of an openly-planned single area with the staff working in close association with the files. The librarian in charge usually occupies a desk in the same room. He is thus immediately available and time and energy is saved when going from desk to filing cabinet and back. The Reuter Library is one of the few where the librarian is installed in a separate office.

There are different practices regarding the relative positions of working area and files. Very few libraries place desks actually among the cabinets, except where the staff specialise in those sections of the library. It would seem better to keep stock and work areas separate, so that desks and tables can be arranged together, perhaps along one side of the room, at right angles to the windows. A frequent arrangement places all the stock in one half of the library area with the staff desks together in the other. Alternatively, one finds the centre of the room occupied by rows of back to back filing cabinets, with the wall space taken up by desks and book stacks.

Where the book collection is of some size the book stacks may be arranged at right angles to the windows so that they act as partitions, dividing the various work sections of the library. The less frequently-used books are sometimes relegated to compact shelving units, as at *The Times*.

The staff need plenty of room to spread themselves, and it is often a problem to prevent the volume of the day's cuttings from engulfing the work space. Desks placed flush against one another or abutting a wall help control the various impedimenta of the cutting process. Markers up need plenty of space to spread out newspapers, and the date stamps and paste pots of the preparatory activity need an equal if not larger amount. Typewriters need desks to themselves, away from the paste and litter. At *The Times* an extra large desk is in use, with lower sliding shelves on which to store telephones. If any indexing is done, this demanding task requires quietness away from the bustle of routine library inquiries.

Room may also be required for shelves of bound newspaper files (at least for the last few years), for extensive trays or volumes of a newspaper index, and for a microfilm reader where appropriate. It is convenient to locate these in association with one another in a less used area of the library, or better, provided supervision is not a problem, in a separate room.

The long term storage of back newspaper volumes occupies so much space that these are frequently stored some distance from the library itself. Space is a precious commodity and, unless the bound files are unusually heavily used, they are likely to be located on another floor—the earliest volumes perhaps in another building. Recent back issues will be available loose in the library.

Provision should be made for quick reference books near the inquiry telephone, for lateral files, and for floor to ceiling shelving for pamphlet boxes and the like.

(iii) FURNITURE AND EQUIPMENT

The most important item of furniture in a news library is the filing equipment for press cuttings. Several basic patterns are in use.

The commonest is the ordinary three or four drawer quarto vertical steel cabinet. The durability and practical success of the vertical file has long since been proved, although, when used to store large quantities of press cuttings, there is undeniably a great waste of 'top space' in the drawers. When lying on their edges, as they do when stored in cabinets, press cuttings—perhaps 4 or 6 in. wide at the most—take up little height, so that approaching half of the vertical space of each cabinet is unoccupied.

Vertical files of five drawers can be supplied standing correspondingly higher, as used by the Press Association for P.A.

copy as well as cuttings. One has seen also banks of two three-drawer cabinets standing on one another. The extreme need to employ space economically is doubtless the reason for this but the plan is hazardous. Open the two top drawers at the same time and, if they are heavy, the whole structure may overbalance forward. Furthermore, apart from the library being turned into a dismal cavern, access to the higher drawers requires the use of short steps, an awkward procedure when carrying a bundle of files.

The libraries of *The Times* and *Daily Mirror*, among others, and many in the United States, solve the wasted drawer space question by using cabinets with shallow (approx. 3 in. or 5 in.) drawers for cuttings. The drawers are deep enough to take single column cuttings laid horizontally on edge. Two or three column stories may be folded to single column width and arranged one behind another. No top space is wasted in the drawers and a large part of the space requirements of quarto cabinets is saved. The drawers being lighter, the cabinets can be stacked to a greater height than would be safe with quarto cabinets. At the *Daily Mirror* such cabinets are employed in eight-drawer units to a height of about 8 ft. Elsewhere, however, it is unusual to find these above 6 ft, and usually less. The tops of the cabinets may thus be used for index trays, pamphlet boxes, and similar items.

While shallow drawers are unbeatable as space economizers, the necessary folding of multi-column cuttings to single-column width renders them tiresome to consult and slower in filing. Inevitably, few cuttings are re-folded before return to the library. In weighing the merits of shallow drawers against quarto size it is worth bearing in mind that shallow drawers do not easily accommodate loose pages from periodicals and other printed information which often proves so useful when filed with press cuttings. At *The Times* the problem is eased by providing next to the cuttings a sequence of drawers containing press handouts and similar transitory material stored flat in a parallel sequence.

In fact, both quarto drawers and shallower ones containing 9 in. × 4 in. files have their place. Smaller drawers save space but are less effective where bulky subjects are concerned. They work well for slender biographical files—but big subjects require big folders.

Another method gaining ground where space is at a premium is the use of lateral filing. Laterals are really a reversion to the old news library method of storing files on shelves like books end on to the user. Files rest within stout folders suspended from rails and lie at right angles to the shelves with only edges showing. A number of variants are now on the market, and all can be moved aside freely to allow the extraction or addition of folders.

Although it has recently been improved by the manufacturers, guiding is still not always as clear as one would like, since there is insufficient space on the visible file edges to display large labels. Further, it is usually necessary to remove files from their position before they can be consulted or before material can be added or replaced. It is in the reserve section for compact storage or for use with special materials like pamphlets or town guides that laterals come into their own. In the reserve section the stacks may be mounted on rails and the banks of files stored closely together, to be pulled apart on their ball-bearing runners as required. No access space is necessary and files can be used up to about eight feet in height. The *Financial Times* library makes effective use of laterals for cuttings and for pamphlets, filing a large amount of material in a remarkably small space. They are similarly employed in the Reuter Library, where quarto files are necessary owing to the Reuter practice of filing Reuter teleprinter messages with cuttings.

Another alternative for cuttings is the use of pamphlet boxes, sometimes known as transfer cases. The most suitable pattern is hinged across one side so that the lid and part of the side fold downwards to allow easy access. Quarto boxes are usually large enough for press cuttings. When made of heavy card or light wood covered with dust-resisting plastic sheeting these form light serviceable receptacles. They can be shelved to any height (being light they are not difficult to lift down) and can be clearly labelled. If necessary, a complete box can be issued. Within the box, cuttings are divided into folders in the normal way or, as at the B.B.C. news library, secured by elastic bands and divided by lightweight paper folders. Similar containers, but larger ($11\frac{3}{4}$ in. × 15 in.) are shelved for cuttings in the library of the Royal Institute of International Affairs. Cuttings are grouped three sheaves to a box, also secured with elastic.

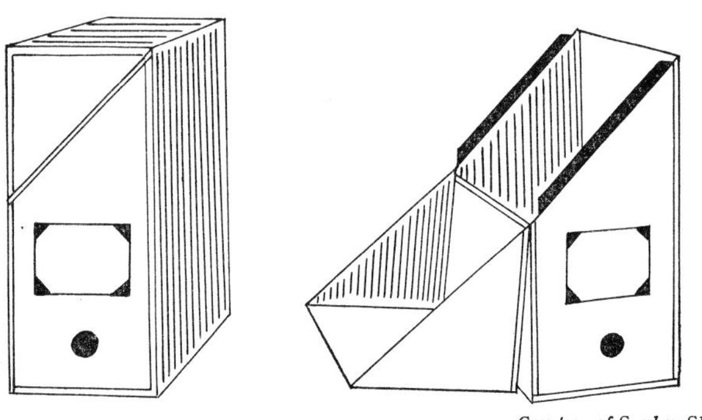

Courtesy of Sankey Sheldon

The lightness of card or wooden boxes unfortunately allows them only a relatively short life, and if heavy wear is likely steel pamphlet boxes should be considered. These have all the advantages of cardboard boxes except lightness and cheapness but they are virtually indestructible. They can be heavy and dangerous to use on high shelves and a number of strategically placed tables and projecting shelves are necessary to rest the boxes on when in use. Steel boxes are quite expensive and even a medium-sized library will require many hundreds of them.

In estimating space requirements and the number of cabinets needed it is important to allow for at least one third expansion. All libraries grow, most of them faster than expected. For the same reason drawers should not be filled to more than two thirds of their capacity. Where boxes are employed, one or two empty containers at the end of each shelf is the ideal.

Once the external filing equipment is chosen, how shall the cuttings be stored inside? There are three basic means: in envelopes, in folders, in nothing. The latter method applies mainly to shallow drawer cabinets where a case can be made out for filing cuttings one behind another, closely packed, and divided only by stiff guide cards. The cards bear tabs raised above the cuttings and each is inscribed with the subject of the cuttings filed behind (or in front of) it. Thus a complete visual index system is in operation and the contents of a drawer and the scope of its headings can be seen at a glance. The snag comes when a number of cuttings are withdrawn for consultation; for they have in any case to be put in some receptacle for issue. The system works best when the cuttings are of uniform column width (i.e. all from the same paper, as at *The Times*).

For use with shallow drawers, not more than 4 in. or 5 in. deep, envelopes with slip tops are better than open-ended folders: they retain the cuttings more securely when removed from the cabinets. The practice of some specific libraries may be of interest. All find their own systems perfectly effective. The Labour Party cuttings are in slit top envelopes, approximately 9 in. × 3½ in., the *Daily Mail* biographical envelopes are slightly larger, 10¾ in. × 3½ in. The *Daily Mirror*, however, uses shallow folders, 10½ in. × 4 in. The *Daily Telegraph* uses gussetted envelopes of quarto size with open top and raised back sheet. The *Telegraph*'s biographical folders, however, are stored in 10 in. × 4 in. containers. *The Guardian* uses quarto manila folders, with open sides, for all material.

Envelopes have the advantage of relative cheapness compared with folders, and, normally, being of thinner material, may be expected to take up less space. They can be reinforced with a canvas lining which, although thickening them slightly, lengthens their life.

They must, of course, be all of the same size: even a slight variation makes rapid leafing through the files more difficult. Additionally, small containers in a larger-sized sequence have a fiendish habit of slipping down between the ranks and disappearing from view.

Envelopes are usually employed like folders, stood on edge with the top edge slit but both sides sealed. They can be bought for use in this form, plus a gusset at the base allowing for expansion. It is necessary where the envelopes are specially made, as we saw with the *Daily Telegraph*, to specify a raised back edge (or part edge) so that the title of each envelope may clearly be read when they are filed one behind another.

There are a number of news libraries using conventional envelopes chiefly of octavo size or smaller, for certain special sequences, stored with an open flap at one side. The obvious disadvantage here, of having to remove each envelope from the sequence before anything can be filed in it, and frequently having to push further items into an envelope already stuffed with cuttings left untidy by the last user, seems overwhelming.

Containers, 9 in. × 4 in., stood vertically on end, are sometimes used side by side in quarto cabinets, two or three rows to a drawer, for little used material, thus making maximum use of the top half of the drawer which is usually wasted in quarto cabinets.

When we consider the enormous range of receptacles now available for cuttings, however, the use of small envelopes acquires a somewhat old-fashioned flavour. Quarto or foolscap cabinets are best used in conjunction with folders, and the office equipment manufacturers have done much to transform this field so that there is now a variety of types available. The conventional open-sided, open-topped folder provides the basis. It can be supplied with one side closed to give extra safety to the contents. Inside pockets for small items or references can be provided. Folders with top edge flaps are a nuisance and only obstruct easy filing and retrieval.

The supreme advantages of the ordinary open-sided folder

when stored in a filing cabinet are ease of access and maximum visibility. The inside contents are not usually secured in any way. Thus new material may be filed by opening a drawer and dropping a cutting in place without removing the folder. Within limits, files themselves may be consulted *in situ*. Unhappily, open-sided folders do occasionally spill their contents when handled carelessly. One just has to learn to hold them upright!

Any assembly of folders stored in vertical files may nowadays expect to be controlled by one or another of the suspended filing systems. For folders which tend to be fat—and in quantity these can be heavy—strong fabric pockets suspended from rigid steel frames within the drawers and guided by raised tabs are suitable. Some types allow the pockets to be removed at will with these acting as folders and, indeed, can make the additional use of folders within the pockets unnecessary. Each pocket bears its label and, if desired, can be used as a folder would be used, remaining always with its contents.

More slender files—those housing a biographical collection, for example—are suitable for storage within a lightweight suspended system incorporating file labels in the suspension rods in a horizontal plane. Suspended pockets of this type are not removable from the main sequence and loose folders have to be used additionally to house the cuttings on issue. Suspension frames are, of course, unnecessary for shallow drawers.

The material used for folders need not be too heavy, for thin card takes up less space. Thick folders wear for ever but get very dirty. There is something to be said for regular replacement of old file containers and if the folder is falling to bits the incentive is the greater.

The correct and imaginative guiding of drawers and files by raised tabs and coloured signals is vitally important where material has to be found quickly. (The headings chosen are referred to in Chapter Ten.) The physical shape and design of the guides varies with the type of files and the office equipment manufacturers offer a wide range of patterns and colours which is still growing. A disadvantage of lateral files is that it is not immediately obvious where a main heading ends and subdivisions begin. The Reuter library uses different colours for main headings and subdivisions on the labels of its lateral files.

Choose the guiding system with care: it must be clear, it must be robust, it should not be too fancy. A good one can make all the difference to the appearance and successful operation of the library.

News libraries do not in general make extensive use of card catalogues and indexes (except possibly for newspaper indexes: Chapter Fourteen). The positioning and selection of a few single trays presents no problem. For private or desk use the simple tray in a cardboard box either 3 in. × 5 in. or 6 in. × 4 in. is quite adequate. If the trays are to be consulted frequently by a variety of people, something stouter is indicated—probably of steel. There are a large number of varieties on the market and metal trays have the advantage of cheapness. Wood is pleasanter to use, but expensive. Whatever type is chosen it is essential in any library that the cards be secured by a rod running the length of the tray and piercing the cards so that they are safe both from over-acquisitive and from clumsy inquirers. Cards should be plain, of the best quality, and rotary cut, for they may be subject to considerable wear over a period of years. If cut with a straight edge the edges tend to blur and stick together.

We have already noted that the remaining furniture of the library should be of generous proportions corresponding to the size of newspapers. The counter will be unusually wide for this reason. Since it will be specially made, opportunity may be taken to provide deep recessed shelves beneath it for loose newspaper files or large reference books.

If the library has a stock of bound newspaper files these will present special storage problems. The excessive weight of bound newspapers (the average weight of a bound volume of *The Times* is 30 lb.) subjects the binding to strain when the volume is stored upright. It is therefore recommended that bound newspapers are stored flat with a maximum of two volumes on each shelf. Slotted shelving allows the necessary passage of air around them. If the shelves are carried on cantilevers, each at the same horizontal level, bound volumes of different dimensions can be placed end to end, some volumes supported by two shelves.

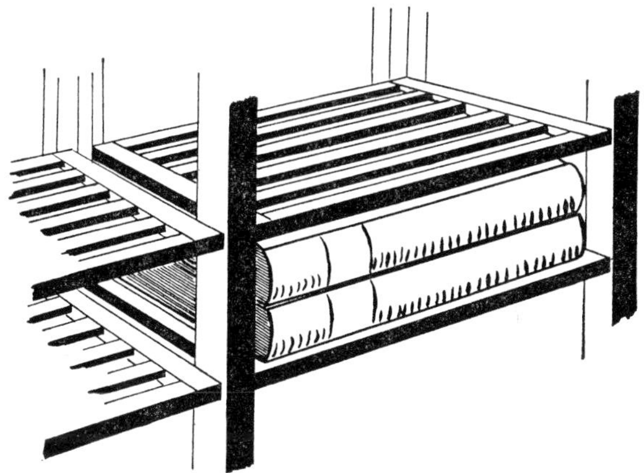

Courtesy of Roneo

This lessens to some degree the prodigal requirement of space which is a disadvantage of shelving flat. (It is a further problem of shelving bound files that they cannot be stored very high since full size newspapers are too heavy to lift down from a height.) If the volumes must be stored vertically, wooden slats between each one or two volumes provide essential support. Otherwise, a number may lean against an early file in the series, wedging it in position and making it almost impossible to remove without first moving away all the volumes leaning against it. The usage of bound files falls off sharply after five or ten years and much space can be saved if the tiers of volumes are mounted on rollers and stored close together, to be easily pushed apart when required. (Care and preservation of bound volumes in Chapter Sixteen.)

The microfilming of back newspaper issues has alleviated but not solved the space problem. Few British newspapers have gone so far as to abandon binding entirely in favour of microfilming. Those which microfilm usually bind also—although probably binding fewer editions. Thus the preservation of microfilm spools and the need for a viewer can create additional demands on space instead of reducing them. Where microfilm is available it will require storage cabinets and a viewer, plus stand and a chair (see Chapter Seventeen).

A useful item of furniture common in older public libraries which seems to be little used by news libraries, is the newspaper slope—a stand at head or waist height with a projecting shelf on the bottom to take a number of newspapers loosely bound. Where wall space is scarce, island slopes are available, which can display newspapers on both sides. *The Times* uses an ingenious system of wall slopes with wide shallow drawers beneath for newspapers less in demand.

Loose newspapers kept for routine reference over short periods are untidy, dog-eared, and a general nuisance, but they are indispensable. Files can be controlled by filing sticks back and front fitted with flexible spikes for impaling new copies each day. The addition of hardboard covers helps the appearance.

The library of a newspaper will certainly require sheet maps. The modern way of storing them, still too little used, is the map cabinet, where they are suspended from horizontal grip bars and available speedily and without the tendency to tearing that comes from storing in large flat drawers. Cabinets are also available for storage horizontally in drawers or in roll form. The *Daily Mirror* stores rolled sheet maps vertically in an 'umbrella stand' designed for the purpose, and has facilities for display on a nearby wall. Folded ordnance survey maps are stored in a cabinet.

Whatever types of equipment—and particularly filing equipment—are chosen, it is of the greatest importance to get it right first time. Considerable capital expenditure is involved and it is unlikely that mistakes can be rectified for many years to come.

Too many librarians are still suffering today from the errors of their predecessors. Time spent on reconnaissance is never wasted and other librarians are usually hospitable. It is true to say, however, that the ideal storage equipment for press cuttings has not yet been invented and there is room for a good deal more research.

As a further view on the matter of accommodation for cuttings, the results of an informal survey of North American newspaper librarians attending the 1964 convention of the Special Libraries Association Newspaper Division may be of interest. Twice as many librarians used shallow drawer equipment in preference to quarto cabinets, and few stored cuttings in open-sided folders. Envelopes were in almost universal use in the libraries of the eighteen librarians replying to a questionnaire. Some envelopes were slit-topped and a large number had a top flap. As might be expected, most libraries use more than one type of equipment.

CHAPTER THREE

The Day's Routine

THE organization of the day's work depends on the number of staff available for the job and the services expected of the library. Larger libraries have a wider scope but they are not necessarily more thorough. The vital tasks of classification and filing are delegated farther down the line and an over-riding problem is to attain consistency of practice from day to day and from assistant to assistant.

The routine work of adding press cuttings to the library may be divided into four simple stages: Selection; Classification; Preparation; Filing.

Obviously, at least two copies of each newspaper from which cuttings are to be taken will be required, so as to cut back and front of pages. Most libraries will need several copies of the papers most important to them so that certain items can be filed in duplicate—under headings concerning more than one point of view.

As we shall see in the next chapter, in the bigger libraries a very large number of newspapers are cut, including multi-copies of the same issue. A limited amount of specialization is possible, so that the sports pages, for example, may be detached and handed over to specialists, and similar treatment may be possible with the foreign news pages of *The Times*.

Selection is a vital job, falling to the senior members of the staff. Each news page is examined, starting at the top of the left-hand column and reading down, a column at a time, through the whole paper. In a very loose way, newspapers organize their news throughout the paper into foreign, home, sport, financial, and so on, each given a separate section. The latest news and perhaps the most important items go on the front or back pages (*The Times* excepted), ignoring this broad classification. So it is possible to cut the job of selection down to size by varying the attention devoted to different parts of the paper. The sports pages, for example, can be ignored in the library not concerned with the subject.

The catholic taste of most general news libraries, however, is sufficiently all embracing to make short cuts unwise and the whole of the editorial must be examined. 'Scanned' or 'looked at' are perhaps better words: there is no time to *read*. The knack of quickly assessing the subject of a news item from the headlines plus the opening paragraph, with only a glance at the remainder, has to be learned. As in other branches of the profession, the news librarian who reads is lost!

The job of selection is called 'marking up' and often it is combined in one operation with classification. Each item to be cut is marked by underlining key words in colour. More complex headings may be written in abbreviated form in the margin. The key word also shows where a cutting came from in case it is separated from its file. Where several copies are needed, they are marked separately with different headings. Some libraries prefer to show the number of copies by a large figure in the margin or in the white space near the headlines.

The importance of marking up fully and classifying intelligently is equalled by the need to ensure absolute consistency. This is not easy in a library working shifts and varying days off. It is essential to record actions and indicate exactly in what way a currently topical subject is being filed. A decisions book should be kept for the purpose, arranged A–Z by subject. The Reuter Library has a good example of this, maintaining a 'drill book' for new staff and others who may forget. A regular library meeting on the subject, attended by the whole staff, is valuable. In order to ensure consistency and avoid duplication, some large libraries advocate marking up all papers and all editions by one person only, however long it takes. He marks broad divisions only; detailed classification is done farther down the line.

Preparation is a routine job and in the larger libraries is done by juniors. Marked up copies of the paper are cut in accordance with the coded instructions. The cuttings are mounted where necessary, marked with the source and date, grouped into alphabetical filing trays, and finally filed with similar items under the appropriate heading. At the press library of the Royal Institute of International Affairs, it is interesting to note, the opposite process takes place. Papers are cut first, then the cuttings are grouped into broad classes on a table divided into sections for the purpose. They are then filed in narrow subject or geographical groups in wall pigeon-holes. From this point, cuttings are finally divided again into their exact place in the classification.

The task occupies a large part of the day and, in topical libraries anyway, should never be allowed to fall behind. Cutting yesterday's papers or papers two or three days old is the dullest job in the world. Consequently, it is never done properly and, in any case, a news library two or three days behind the times is not doing its job.

In a library open round the clock the day staff will deal with the morning editions and those coming on duty later with the evening papers plus anything left over by their predecessors. A news library serving a morning paper needs to have the greater part of its routine cleared by mid-afternoon so that free time is available for the peak level of inquiries which usually flow in a few hours before first edition time—10 or 11 p.m.

Much argument is engendered over the best tools for cutting newspapers. Some think they are best cut with a safety razor blade, working through one sheet at a time on a cutting board. Cheap metal guards are on sale to prevent fingers being lopped off.

Tailor's scissors, steel and plastic rulers for tearing against, all have their protagonists. It is a matter of what you get used to. If forced to express an opinion, one might opt for a guarded razor blade on the grounds that it is neater and quicker in use.

There is a case for not cutting streamer headlines employed by some papers, extending often across seven columns for a one or two column story, and filing the body of the text only. Judged from the severe standards of reference, headlines can be misleading and the true subject of a news item can sometimes be more easily arrived at with their distracting influence absent. On the other hand, it must be admitted that many inquirers after a particular news item carry a visual memory of it consisting mainly of the headline, and its omission may make the item more difficult to identify.

Whether or not to mount press cuttings is a decision each library must reach, having regard to the type of newspaper normally cut. The *New York Times* and *The Guardian* libraries do not mount, because they cut principally their own newspaper where one or two-column stories with straightforward layout stand perfectly well without mounts. *The Guardian* and some other libraries mount a small number of tiny news items (less than 2 or 3 column inches).

Other libraries with large quantities of cuttings from the narrow columns of the *Daily Telegraph* or the *Daily Sketch* find some form of backing essential. The *Financial Times* mounts everything on quarto-sized white paper, the sheets secured to the folder by a 'bootlace' threaded through the top left hand corner. It is usual to employ white or coloured newsprint for mounts which is cheap and also thin, so reducing to a minimum the virtual doubling of space requirements needed by mounted cuttings. Bank paper is satisfactory but expensive.

Overall backing for items of perhaps a column length being impracticable on a large scale, mountings usually take the form of a standard sized sheet of newsprint (sometimes only a tab) to which the top inch or so of the cutting is pasted. Mounting sheets are best prepared in one or two standard sizes with room for date and source of the news item. Long single column cuttings must be folded under the top section. To leave the bottom piece loose and dangling is asking for it to be torn off in a short time. The library of *The Times* uses gummed slips of exactly column width with space for source and date entries.

Cuttings are usually pasted to mounts. Here and there a strip of plastic tape is used instead: neat but expensive on a large scale. White paste does a neater job than brown—and both should be used sparingly so as to avoid the horror of damp and gluey cuttings sticking to one another. A paste brush is necessary: the patent rubber dispensers in the form of bottle caps are too slow in use. 'Poppet pens' charged with a latex adhesive are effective within limits.

It is a sound practice to change the colour of the mounts each year as is done at the *Daily Mirror*, *The Times*, and elsewhere. Cuttings out of order will be quickly noted, and discarding is

Councillors will visit 'twist and shout' session

Councillors at Beaumaris, in Anglesey, are to visit a "twist and shout" session because they want to hear whether the pounding of beat groups and the stamping of feet is creating too much noise.

There have been a number of complaints about the noise coming from weekly dances at the Town Hall, and Mr David Senogles, the town clerk, explained yesterday that the councillors wanted to judge for themselves.

Courtesy of The Guardian

made easier when the time comes. Another use of coloured mounts is to indicate which section of the library (Biography, Sport, etc.) a cutting belongs to. In this way a cutting replaced in the wrong section clamours for attention. The Royal Institute of International Affairs uses yellow mounts to indicate cuttings from *The Times* and pink ones to indicate official communiques and terms of agreements.

Whether mounted or not, the source and date of each cutting must be indicated. This is best done by a specially-made rubber stamp, incorporating the date with the initials of several alternative newspapers. Alternatively, a selection of gummed tabs or mounting slips may be printed in advance with the name of each newspaper taken in the library and used with the appropriate date as is done at the B.B.C.

The cuttings, dated and bearing the source abbreviation, will already carry the classification heading indicated by the marker

Pakistani aid for £1.8 m. Nigerian jute industry

A new £1.8 millions jute industry is to be set up jointly in Nigeria by the Pakistan and Northern Nigeria Governments, following a recent Pakistan trade delegation to the country. The leader of the Pakistan delegation commented that his Government decided on the venture because Northern Nigeria consumed well over 60 per cent of Pakistan jute exports, and the climate was very good for jute production.

Courtesy of The Guardian

up. The next task is to divide them into two piles—those which can be filed immediately with headings already in use and those which require new files.

A number of new files will be made every day as new subjects and people spring into prominence. Each new heading is the subject of careful consideration (see Chapter Ten). The preparation of a new file entails inscribing the heading clearly along the visible edge. The heading should start at the left and be large enough to be clearly read. Typewriters are to be got which will type 18 or 24 point headings. Indian ink is better and someone trained in freehand lettering is a great help, although clear writing with a lettering nib is a skill that can be acquired. Where major headings are added it should not be overlooked that the cabinet guides will probably need amendment also. If an index or schedule of subject headings in use is maintained it is most important that every new subject heading should be entered in it.

The physical job of filing is simple. Economical organization demands that cuttings awaiting filing are first sorted into alphabetical order in the same sequence as the file headings. According to the daily quantity to be filed, it may be useful to employ an alphabetical book or concertina of folders, or a series of baskets on wheels for moving round the library. It is, of course, vital to file accurately. A cutting misplaced is a cutting lost. It is never found until too late.

Each new cutting is filed in the front of its sequence so that the contents are kept in chronological order. When a file is removed, laid flat, and opened, the cuttings may be turned over and read like the pages of a book, with the latest on top. Some items, such as summaries or lists, are occasionally more important for themselves than as part of the chronological sequence. These may be separated and pasted or otherwise affixed in a prominent position near the face of the file as permanent contributions to the subject, facilitating quick reference.

Any news library prides itself on being absolutely up to date. To achieve this ideal a constant watch is necessary, not only for new subjects, but for the changes undergone by old ones. Many of these will require new names to keep up with changes in terminology. Companies change their names, so do countries and towns (Zambia, Iran, Irish Republic, Dolwyddelan). Atomic Bombs become Hydrogen Bombs, Public Assistance becomes National Assistance, Reformatories become Approved Schools, Distressed Areas become Development Areas, and so on.

It is worse with people. The marriage of a prominent woman will entail the replacement of her earlier with her later name, unless she remains better known by some other name. The twice-yearly Honours Lists impose a huge task on a library endeavouring to keep an extensive biographical section up to date. Elevations to the peerage often result in a complete change of name, as well as of title. Promotions of members of the armed forces or the clergy all need recording on the outside as well as the inside of a file where a change of title is involved. Few things cause more annoyance than to refer to a baron as a knight, overlooking that he was raised to the peerage in the last Honours List. It is almost as unfortunate to be premature and refer to a commoner as a knight before he has received the accolade.

These lapses in published references are rightly traced back to an inefficient library information service. Library terminology must keep up with current usage, and nothing undermines confidence so quickly as dated headings. It is a daily job, therefore, to remove from the files those headings which require amendment and to see that these are dealt with promptly. Deaths must be recorded with scrupulous care and the outside of the file clearly marked 'DIED . . .' and the date. Removal of the file to a separate sequence of dead or historic files helps to avoid error but, whether or not this is done, it is good practice to draw two firm lines diagonally across the outside of the file indicating that its personality is dead. It is all too easy to confuse (say) the biographical file of the 3rd Baron with that of his dead father, the 2nd Baron.

At this point it may be appropriate to comment on the value

of other sources of information in keeping the collection up to date—particularly the biographical section. It cannot be too often said that it is not the library's job to supply press cuttings so much as to supply information. Other sources than the routine cutting of the normal daily press can be made use of.

For example, the lists of promotions and service changes in the *London Gazette* should be examined. So should the obituary notices and appointments columns of *The Times* and *Financial*

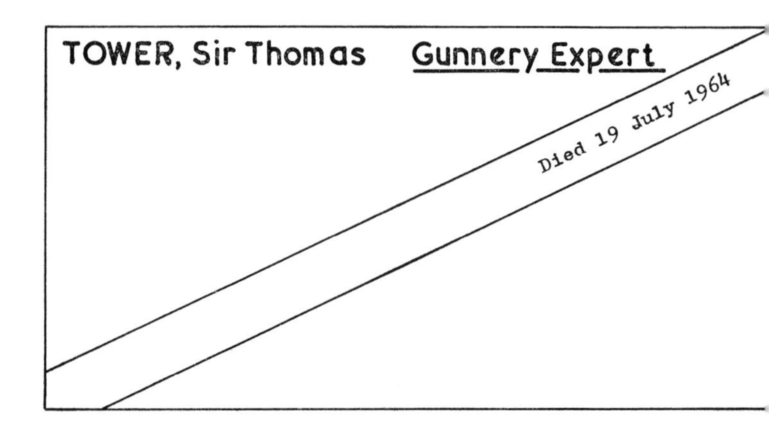

Times. It is a wise safeguard to include in the day's routine a check of the names mentioned there against the biographical files. In the case of obituary notices a good many deaths which might otherwise be overlooked can be noted in this way. The point here is often not so much that of collecting information as of enabling the weeding of unimportant files which, where they have contained perhaps a single cutting of no great importance, can now be destroyed. Further, it is a sad fact that to establish with certainty from files whether a person who has dropped out of the news is now alive or dead, is often no easy matter.

It sometimes becomes necessary to close a file on other

grounds. Files which have grown too fat and do not lend themselves to subdivision by subject may be divided chronologically. It is important not to allow folders or envelopes to become overstuffed with cuttings. Whatever carefully chosen system is in operation it is soon ruined if files are choked with too much material, thus obstructing rather than assisting the search for information. However narrow the subject matter or otherwise apparently indivisible, it is always possible to divide chronologically.

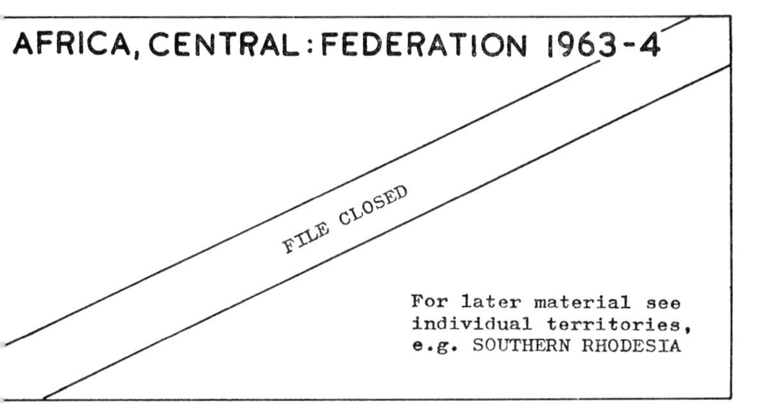

A clear indication on the outside of a file that it is closed is necessary to prevent material accidently being filed in it. One useful way of achieving this is by means of a coloured sticker, perhaps a bright red star or something similar, on the visible part of the file as it stands in its sequence.

Files bearing similar headings should be clearly marked on the outside

BEWARE SIMILAR NAME

or

SHAW, Councillor Albert, *Labour.* Do not confuse with
SHAW, Councillor Albert, *Conservative*

so as to ensure as far as possible that confusion will not arise when a file is sought in a hurry.

Undoubtedly, some inaccurate or contentious items do get in to the press from time to time. When these come to the notice

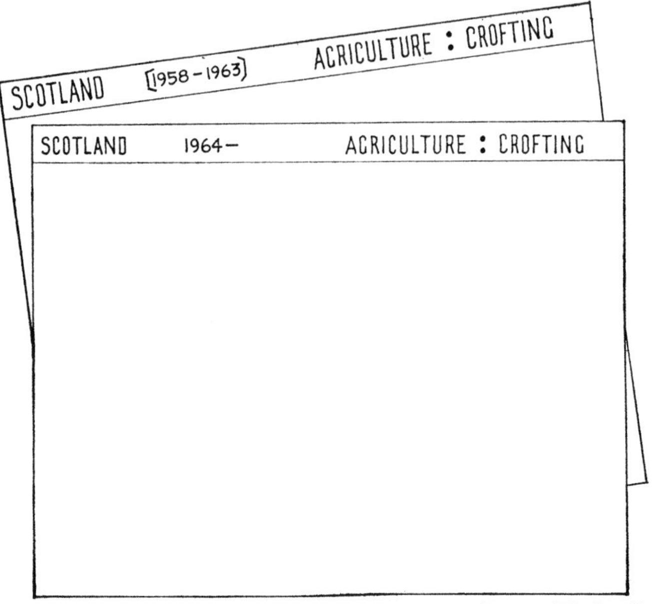

Courtesy of The Guardian

of the library the greatest care must be taken. The *Daily Mirror* keeps such cuttings but overprints each one

DO NOT QUOTE or REFER TO LEGAL DEPT

The Press Association library prints a warning in large red letters on all its folders:

WARNING

IN USING THESE CUTTINGS, IN ADDITION TO CROSS CHECKING ON DOUBTFUL DETAILS OR DISCREPANCIES, EXTREME CARE SHOULD BE TAKEN TO SEE

THAT NO INNUENDO IS SET UP BY REASON OF THE JUXTAPOSITION OF 'LIVE COPY' AND DETAILS FROM CUTTINGS. SATISFY YOURSELF THAT THE CUTTINGS YOU USE, FROM WHATEVER SOURCE, ARE FREE FROM POSSIBLE LIBEL.

Before filing, the number of new files added should be noted. In this way a working total of the number of files in the library is maintained—a piece of information demanded now and again for insurance purposes and also useful to the librarian anxiously watching the rate of growth of his library.

The files stored away, let us consider their issue and return. Where a counter is in use it is advisable that someone should be on duty at that point. Much of the work of issuing files and recording their return will fall to him, as will numerous inquiries from the telephone at his side. We have already made provision for a selection of quick reference books near the counter, but inquiries demanding an intensive search may be passed on elsewhere.

Ensuring the safe return of material on loan occupies much time and effort in most libraries. The process begins with recording its issue. The simplest system is the issue book, of course, ruled into columns for the date, form and subject of the material, borrower's signature, date of return, and so forth.

It is interesting to note that insistence on a personal signature from everyone borrowing material is a strong psychological encouragement to return it. Merely to enter the name of the borrower is not nearly so effective. Most libraries endeavour to enforce a rule insisting that all material is returned the same day and a check of the issue book on the following morning is all that is necessary to chase up defaulters. Entries for material kept longer than a day may be carried forward day by day until cleared.

The issue book works less well, however, when a large amount of material is retained over longer periods. It might be considered then whether a flag signalling card index system were not

DATE	ITEM	BORROWER'S SIGNATURE	CHECKED	REPLACED

worth while, of which a number are on the market. This may be combined with the use of requisition slips on which inquirers list the material they need and append their names. (The signatures of messengers are not acceptable.) The slips may be used in duplicate: one copy is left in the file in the place of cuttings (or folders) removed and the other is filed under a date system in a slip index of material on loan.

The *Philadelphia Inquirer* library uses triplicate slips tipped together at the left-hand edge, of white, blue, and yellow. On issuing material the white slip goes in the file from which material is removed and stays there until it is returned. This shows what is out and who has it. The blue slip goes out with the material. This identifies what is in the library's special out-charge folders and for whom it is intended. The yellow slip is kept in date file as a record of what is out. It is discarded when the white slip is removed from the file and matched with it on the return of the material.

Whether or not such a system is used in full, it is highly desirable that whenever a file is removed from its sequence something remains in place of it to indicate its absence. A strong coloured card, slightly higher than the files, merely saying OUT is often sufficient. The *Daily Telegraph* uses a green card for the purpose. The flagging of files on loan is important, since, on newspapers anyway, it is not uncommon for a reporter and a sub-editor to require the same file at the same time (or, more likely, for the reporter to be late returning it!).

The problem is more difficult when a single cutting, or just a small number, are loaned instead of the whole file. A number of libraries, in fact, never lend files—only a selection of cuttings from files. A single press cutting is a vulnerable object and the fact that it is missing from among others on the same subject is not always apparent. It only becomes disastrously evident—too late—when it is wanted. Therefore such lonely items need special protection.

The question is dealt with at the *Daily Telegraph* by removing the file from its sequence whenever anything is taken from it, and placing it in a special basket to await the return of loaned items. The borrowed cuttings are issued in large coloured envelopes, too big to lose, heavily printed RETURN TO LIBRARY. The file's proper position in the sequence is flagged OUT, and the folder awaits return of part of its contents. Only when cuttings are returned and replaced is the folder put back into sequence and its return recorded.

It must sadly be confessed, however, that success in persuading users to fill in forms and otherwise record their borrowings is hard to come by. Before replacement—a job which, in newspaper libraries, can be done late at night when the rush of inquiries has ceased—the contents of returned files or envelopes must be checked. No one has as yet devised a practical way of ensuring that each of perhaps 100 cuttings has been returned. Life is too short to count them in and out. Nevertheless, important or familiar items missing may be evident.

It is well that borrowers returning material to the library should know exactly where to put it. For this purpose, and to ensure that, once returned, files do not go astray before being checked off, a 'returned files' box should be installed. Placed in a prominent position near the counter, it should be emptied regularly and a daily routine established for returning files to the sequence.

As part of a continuous programme of the collection of information and documents of all kinds there is something to be said in publishing and news organizations for establishing library boxes at various strategic points in other departments. Editorial people handle large quantities of documents, many of them thrown away unused. If they can be persuaded instead to drop them in a box for consideration by the library as possible additions, something is gained.

CHAPTER FOUR

Selection

This is not the place to consider which newspapers to cut, nor precisely what subjects. Each library collects according to experience of past demand—and the more sensitive it is to user requirements the more successful its service is likely to be. It will be appropriate if we consider in this chapter the practice of the general news library. Even these vary in their needs.

The library of Reuter's News Agency naturally concentrates on foreign news (although British home news is also cut) while the complementary service provided by the Press Association for United Kingdom news requires a library slanted towards home affairs, cutting the provincial papers as well as the nationals. The national daily and Sunday papers and the radio and television news service libraries are perhaps the most wide ranging—some of them attempting to cover everything.

In Fleet Street the *Daily Telegraph* cuts every news item published in its own columns and employs some 70 copies of its own paper for the purpose. Other nationals are cut only lightly. At one time the *Daily Mirror* indexed its own columns and filed cuttings from other papers. Now everything is cut from the *Mirror* and other nationals, plus a number of provincials and periodicals. The range continually grows wider. *The Times* relies chiefly on its own cuttings and its printed *Index*, the two jobs being carried out independently. In addition, *The Times* has maintained for some sixty years a series of bound cuttings books, wherein *The Times* cuttings are mounted and arranged by subject, thus providing a convenient source of reference from their own columns and enabling the basic cuttings sequence to be weeded more drastically. *The Guardian* indexes its own editorial exhaustively and maintains a substantial selection of its own and other people's news cuttings. The Reuter Library is principally a key to the Reuter copy, but *The Times*, the *New York Times*, and the *Herald Tribune* are also cut.

The libraries of many British provincial papers, since they publish the Reuter and P.A. news services with minimum editing, ignore much foreign and home political news and concentrate on local events. (The better provincial newspaper libraries, incidentally, provide a magnificent source for recent local history, particularly where, as it should, the press library works closely with the local reference library.)

Nevertheless, no news library, however localized, can safely forego collecting biographical information and a certain amount of general reference material. Provision must be made for collecting information not only on the specific field with which the library is mainly concerned, but for coping with the wider range of inquiries which any library attracts simply because it is there.

Those libraries which cut everything, or nearly everything, have many problems, but selection is not one of them. For the rest, a choice has to be made. But which to choose? Experience is the only guide. The most important rule is 'Will it be needed again?', which should not be interpreted as 'It might come in useful some day', a view which is the refuge of the over-cautious librarian who soon finds his library clogged with valueless cuttings. Over-zealous selection can be almost as bad as cutting too little and the search for a single item can be fatally obstructed by a mass of unnecessary material.

In other words, the cuttings chosen should be judged on the meat in them. Figures and facts, statements which may be referred to later, actual decisions and actions—these are what are required. Some newspapers, particularly *The Times*, publish from time to time a summary of events or facts on a topical subject which represent the kind of presentation to be watched for.

News is principally about people and consequently biography looms large in the coverage of a news library. People are alive and changing and doing things. Even those meriting entries in the published reference sources of contemporary biography, such as *Who's Who* and the like, are never adequately covered by these alone. A collection of cuttings is essential to provide the latest information and give more detail than the reference books. Many subject cuttings have a biographical aspect also and this should never be overlooked when selecting the day's news cuttings. Not only a man's personal life, but some form of reference to all the topics with which he is concerned, is an indispensable part of the library's coverage.

Depending on the coverage expected of the library a decision will be made in regard to foreign and international news. The decision must take into account what other sources of information are available. It may be that *Keesing's Contemporary Archives* will be found sufficient, particularly if there are other good libraries near by or reachable by telephone.

If foreign affairs are important to the library, all must be cut. There is no way of distinguishing the important from the trivial. Some may feel able to ignore reports of small incidents in a trouble spot, but such arbitrary decisions can be dangerous.

War news is difficult: so many operational reports are quickly superseded by contradictory details. During the Second World War most libraries found it necessary to create a separate section of the library devoted to the subject and made a selection from the enormous mass of published material. The problem was made easier by the dearth of news of most other topics and by the smallness of newspapers. Nowadays war is most conveniently treated as part of the foreign affairs of the country in which the fighting takes place, and a separate subdivision devoted to it, e.g.:

KOREA: WAR: OPERATIONS
LAOS: OPERATIONS

Topical news of wars—and particularly of military operations—is frequently vague and often misleading. It is seldom needed for long. Summaries and statements some time after the event should be watched for. It is convenient where possible to keep military operations separate from the rest, not so much that the news is valuable in itself but so that the sheer volume of news about battles is not allowed to obstruct the more frequent need for reference to political aspects of war news. Minor reports of patrol activities, aircraft sorties, and so on may largely be ignored. Rumours, however, should be retained for a time at least, for it is impossible to forecast how they may develop. The value of one newspaper's war section is shown by the library of *The Times*, which was consulted by Sir Winston Churchill's researchers when he was writing his war memoirs.

News about the armed forces breaks down into: the strength and disposition of armies, fleets and air forces, methods of training, weapons, uniforms, recruiting, and so forth. In particular, the general newspaper library will keep abreast of rank and decorations of senior personnel.

Parliamentary news is usually well-documented and verifiable. Political news is not. Since the proceedings of both Houses of Parliament are recorded verbatim, a subscription to the daily or weekly *Hansard* may be sufficient. *Hansard* (although indexed) is not an easy publication for quick reference, and it may well be that the subject filing of *The Times* parliamentary page provides a good answer for most news libraries. The press report is concise, its contents is guided by cross-heads, and each debate or parliamentary question can be filed according to the library's own scheme of arrangement.

Parliamentary news is mainly speeches, and speeches are of great importance to news libraries. The library is continually being asked: 'When did Churchill refer to the Iron Curtain?'; 'Who made a reference to "grouse moor" politics?' or 'What exactly did the Prime Minister say about butter and the Common Market?' Such remarks made in the course of speeches in either

House are traceable. Many speeches, however—of the Duke of Edinburgh, for instance—which may frequently be referred to later, are made elsewhere and appear nowhere else than in newspapers. Clearly, if the library anticipates a demand, they must not be missed and should be cut in the fullest version available. The value of a good speeches collection was proved at the library of the Royal Institute of International Affairs which was called upon to provide evidence from the speeches of the Nazi war leaders to be used at the Nuremberg trials.

In addition to filing political speeches, most general libraries find it necessary to maintain records of general party policy statements and to file, with the topics of the day, party political pronouncements on them.

A problem of some difficulty from the point of view of selection is election news—or, rather, pre-election news. The larger part of the words written about the great debate, whether it be local or national—are of only the most transitory interest. To meet a demand everything may have to be filed—but only until the election is over—and it is worth considering whether this kind of temporary material may not be kept under broad headings in a separate section of the library, to be heavily weeded and transferred to the permanent collection later. There is a purely physical problem here. Such temporary subjects can be of enormous passing interest and the volume of cuttings quickly outgrows the available space for it in the main sequence. It is not worth a major move round to make space because the files will be drastically reduced in size before very long.

The activities of government departments influence our lives and are always a basis of inquiries. New legislation, the scheduling of national parks and historic buildings, education proposals, motoring laws, taxation, budget proposals are just a few examples of essential items. Furthermore, the press report is often easier to understand than the official document. It is also necessary to have readily available the latest composition of the Cabinet ('Who is the new Secretary of State for Scotland?') and changes in other senior government posts. In those libraries concerned with them the present composition of foreign governments is also important ('Who has taken over in Zanzibar?'). The Reuter Library maintains an excellent and up-to-date list of foreign governments on Roneodex cards amended daily.

Industrial news, production figures by industries, exports and imports, wages and prices, food and agriculture, fuel and power, all these and similar subjects are obvious pillars of the stock of the general news library. Provincial libraries will naturally concentrate on the local aspects of the same subjects. For them the Town Hall takes the place of the Houses of Parliament and the Lord Mayor the Prime Minister. All local aspects of social welfare and local industries will be covered, *Whitaker's Almanack*, the *Monthly Digest of Statistics*, and *Keesing's* perhaps sufficing for the rest. Attention should also be paid to the constitution, membership, and activities of societies. A.G.M. reports are useful, particularly if officials are referred to by name.

News about entertainment and the arts falls into three main categories—biographical, critical, and, to a lesser degree, financial aspects. Many general news libraries require to file all play or film reviews—even pre-views, which are useful to the reviewer. Further, it is often helpful to know the dates and cast lists of earlier performances. Television, the cinema, books, and so forth can, of course, be treated entirely as commercial subjects, from the economic point of view, as is done in the library of the *Financial Times*.

Most news libraries, however, will treat (say) television from all these standpoints, keeping news about personalities and programmes, with a separate section on television policies and finance. Programme reviews and minor criticisms are seldom worth keeping for long, although in provincial libraries a decision will have to be made about the filing of local exhibition and concert reports. One-man shows may be of biographical interest, book reviews may be regarded as belonging in the biographical file of their author or as a contribution to the subject under review.

All major accidents and disasters should be filed, for they are long remembered and may be needed for comparisons. These include railway, road, aeroplane and domestic accidents, shipwrecks, fires, explosions, earthquakes, and most of the other fatalities to which mankind is subject. It is difficult to know where to draw the line. While it is usually unnecessary to keep every small untoward occurrence reported in the newspapers, one must have some kind of guide to selection. Some libraries file only fatal accidents—which presumably entails waiting to see if the victim dies before making a decision. Others notice only those involving financial loss above a certain level—which is open to similar objections. In general, only experience can decide if a report is likely to be remembered again and, bearing in mind the pressure on space, it is wise to be sparing of selection in this field.

In a similar category are disasters attributable to the weather—floods, tornadoes, droughts, freak storms, etc. Most of these are worth keeping, since the weather is a perennial topic. Figures are needed of temperature, rainfall, sunshine, and wind, with comparisons.

Crime is a subject of importance in any news library for two reasons. First, because it is a subject of permanent public interest and, second, because it is seldom recorded elsewhere than in the press. Murder and manslaughter, kidnapping, blackmail, large scale robbery, all attract great attention and should be filed in detail. On the other hand, many of the cases tried in the lower courts may be ignored. As with reports of accidents, some rule of thumb is required, giving guidance on selection. Apart from the cases of great national interest, the general run of crime reports are not wanted again. Statistics can best be gathered from blue books. Sometimes the news library may be asked to file a certain class of crime or accident, e.g. mail bag robberies or railway accidents involving faulty signals, under this special aspect, using the material for a campaign later. Further, as with other subjects involving personal names, it is sound practice to check them against existing files. More than once a new and unexpected angle has been provided on a story in this way.

Civil actions are too variable to allow dogmatism but the more dramatic of them (some libel actions, for instance) are long remembered and quoted. *The Times* law reports are the most authoritative in this connexion.

If sport is to be filed the subject requires specialised treatment. Apart from tables of results, reigning champions, records, and the domestic affairs of clubs, sport is mainly a biographical subject. Sporting personalities are treated in the same way as other prominent people, but most of the commentaries, match descriptions, forecasts, and discussions of form are valueless to the library. A clear line must be drawn between the permanent and the transitory, depending on the demand made of the library. Both the high value placed on sports news by editors and the difficulty of finding good reference books makes it important for the news library. On the other hand, few topics are so extensively written about with so little lasting value.

All cuttings describing the history of localities, buildings and geographical features, including, of course, recent developments, are useful, particularly if they contain plenty of facts and figures and are not merely laudatory. The heights of mountains and of buildings, the depths of seas and mines, the lengths of bridges, rivers, and similar statistics, are of inexhaustible interest. For the same reason it is important to look out for records of all kinds—the fastest train, ship, or bicycle, the farthest and the heaviest, the first and the last, and so on.

We have referred more than once to news library's emphasis on biography. Chief among this class is news about royal personages of all countries. To cut and classify in detail the court circular in *The Times* is seldom necessary, but all major journeys should be documented, plus all royal speeches. Succession questions and family relationships are often difficult and, since most news about the British Royal family is only to be found in newspapers, press cuttings assume more than ordinary importance.

Much of the foregoing applies also to political leaders and prominent people in all walks of life. Popular journalism requires voluminous background material on the personalities of the day—entertainers, 'top people', the notorious, and so forth, about whom the press is often the only published source of information.

Oddities, freaks, and events of interest only because of their strangeness should not be scorned; they are frequently of use simply because of their oddity. It is surprising how in a short space of time a collection of curious facts on a subject can be gathered from daily newspapers, to be used later, perhaps, in a feature. Many of the famous *Times* 'fourth leaders' are produced in this way.

All depends, of course, on demand. At the library of the *Financial Times* company meeting reports are basic stock. The provincial library will ignore them if they are not local.

For the newspaper library, the home newspaper's opinions, as expressed in its leading articles, and any of its pronouncements elsewhere, will certainly qualify for retention. Sometimes special means of filing, classifying by 'form' as well as by subject, are required for these.

Which topics may safely be ignored is only learned from the nature of the inquiries made to the library. Smaller libraries ignore random letters to the editor, for example, except perhaps when a large number are published on some burning issue. Forecasts of the probable trend of affairs and of forthcoming events are rarely worth keeping beyond the date they refer to. Conference reports tend to be remembered only for a short time —the resolutions are the library's chief concern, unless some speech makes an important contribution to the subject. Announcements of forthcoming entertainments, sporting fixtures, and the like fall into the unwanted category unless required as a record of 'coming events'. Advertisements are only occasionally regarded as potential library material—such items as share issue advertisements and special announcements are useful.

Unimportant births, marriages, divorces, deaths, and wills may be ignored after the names have been checked against existing files. Stock exchange share movements will not be wanted after the day of publication unless some startling boom or collapse brings them on to the front page. Most fashion articles can be ignored, unless the library is specially concerned with the subject. A large number of children's and youth features, competitions and cartoons are valueless to the library.

Usually, more than one newspaper is examined, though the burden of cutting will fall mainly on the first read. Naturally, this will be the one with the most comprehensive coverage in the field required. Most newspaper libraries find it necessary to have a complete file or index to the contents of all editions of the home newspaper. Irrespective of their value as contributions to the subject, therefore, these items will be given priority. It should be remembered that newspapers are published in several editions and some items appear only in one. If complete coverage is required it is necessary to examine all editions, starting with the latest, and cut from the earlier editions items dropped from later ones.

After this, other papers are read for items not carried in the first and for stories giving more information on a current subject. It is not possible to check in detail one story's coverage against another, so, in general, it must suffice to keep the longest. It will be found necessary to read with care only two or three newspapers, the remainder may be scanned, paying special attention to the subjects in which each specializes, and looking out for exclusives.

In the search for information periodicals are not overlooked and, provided the filing equipment is suitable, whole articles can be cut out and filed with cuttings. A magazine article, like a newspaper feature, may be useful in summarizing, saving time which would otherwise be spent later in collecting facts from several places.

A library serving an organization concerned with mass communication is in a fortunate position, for it attracts printed matter of all kinds. Press 'hand-outs' may occasionally be useful, even if they are not used elsewhere. At election times candidates' manifestos contain useful biographical material. Commercial advertisement brochures indicate the size and scope of local industries. House journals not worth filing in their entirety may contain useful articles, and even the humble parish magazine usually lists the name of the incumbent and various addresses and telephone numbers. In the field of entertainment and leisure there is something to be said for collecting theatre programmes for the cast list and story outline, and many librarians find it useful to obtain film synopses from cinema managements. Other sources of information worth watching for are the dust covers of books received for review. Frequently a biographical note on the author is to be found there, information not always easy to come by if the writer is not well known.

While every experienced librarian is on his guard against his library being used as a dustbin whence anything unwanted may be retrieved or, in other words, be used as a safeguard by the over-cautious who dread throwing anything away, it is wise to encourage the offer of material by library users, while retaining the option of discarding it if useless. In this way, a large part at any rate of the printed matter reaching the library's parent organization is eventually considered for use by the library.

CHAPTER FIVE

General Arrangement

THE *potential* value of the library is related to the volume of cuttings and other printed matter it holds. Its *actual* efficiency is dependent on the way in which this material is arranged, and the speed and success with which accurate and complete information can be produced. After the all-important matter of correct and imaginative selection therefore everything depends on a first-class arrangement. What is the best method?

For a highly specialized library, or one which regards cuttings as supplementary to the main stock, there is something to be said for arranging cuttings in the same way as the rest of the collection—the Universal Decimal Classification, for example, or a local scheme designed for a particular subject.

In the case of general news libraries, however, other considerations apply, influenced by the physical shape of press cuttings, their approach to the subject dealt with, the type of the inquiry the news library is designed to answer, and the way news is divided up in the mind of the inquirer. Press cuttings are different in nature from books and their range is wider. In addition, they are generally much more specific and require narrower subdivision. It is true that one cutting may cover several subjects, like a book, but whereas a book can only be classified in one place (usually the general, or embracing subject), for a press cutting this would be wrong. The problem can be solved by filing several copies. (See Chapter Eight.)

The news library being principally an information service based on press cuttings, inquiries may take any of three forms: they may be for a specific piece of information, for a specific remember cutting (out of hundreds of thousands), or a request for a whole file on a subject for background reading. Speed is necessary, too, and arrangement becomes primarily a finding device.

The qualities required of the scheme of arrangement may be summed up as:

Easy to understand and remember
Simple to operate
Speedy access to information
Permitting entrance of new subjects with full prominence
Allowing for change of heading or emphasis when appropriate.

Most news libraries have independently come to the conclusion that the scheme best fulfilling these conditions is a straightforward alphabetical series of main headings, each subdivided alphabetically where necessary.

The alphabet is easily remembered and understood and subject headings in full describe their scope right away without any key being required. In contrast to a scheme using letters or numbers as symbols the system can be extended and altered indefinitely without arbitrary restrictions imposed by the limitations of 10 numbers or 26 letters.

In the smallest library it is perfectly practicable—and probably desirable—to use one sequence for all cuttings. People, places, and other subjects are each classified as minutely as possible under direct headings; subdivision is kept to a minimum. Each cutting is filed under the narrowest heading which will contain it and the headings are grouped in a single alphabetical sequence. This is the order of a general encyclopaedia and results in the following:

FIELDS, Gracie
FINLAND
FISHER, Dr Geoffrey
FISHING INDUSTRY
FLAGS

The system gives maximum simplicity and enables the library to be consulted effectively by untrained inquirers without the assistance of the library staff. Associated subjects may be widely separated according to the accident of their initial letter and no attempt is made (except through references) to relate (say) OYSTERS to other shellfish. This is not regarded in such libraries as an important disadvantage.

As the collection grows, some subjects throw up special problems which are best dealt with by grouping them together. One of these is biography. News about people is so predominant in press cuttings that it is normally given a section of its own. Similar separate sequences may be established for cuttings about places—consisting of those items where locality interest outweighs national or subject interest. These include local government and topographical and historical information. (See Chapter Seven.) The B.B.C. News Library contains such a section, simply entitled PLACES, although the section includes many subjects filed under place for convenience of finding. News about foreign countries is similarly given a special section where the name of the country is the main heading, as in the B.B.C. and Labour Party libraries.

One of the most frequently used arrangements divides the library into three main sections:

General
Foreign
Biography

although there is a variety of possible permutations, as can be shown by reference to the basic arrangement of certain news libraries.

The libraries of the Press Association and *The Guardian*, for example, have only two main sequences: Biography and the remainder, so that British place names and foreign countries come directly under their own names in the alphabetical sequence. The *Evening News* library, which formerly served the

News Chronicle and *Star* (now defunct), has a similar arrangement, starting at AALAND ISLANDS and going on through AERONAUTICS, COLDS, ESPIONAGE to ZULULAND. The *Daily Telegraph* has General, Places, and Personal, with English places under ENGLAND and Austrian news under AUSTRIA in the same Places sequence. The *Daily Mirror* library is divided into General, Geographical, and Biography. General includes special sections such as Crime, Sport, and Entertainment, which are virtually separate collections. Like the *Telegraph*, the *Mirror's* Geographical Section includes British places under Britain in the same sequence as other countries. *The Times* has Subjects, Foreign, Places (English), and Biography.

Various other sequences are found reflecting the needs of the library users. There is danger, however, in forming too many main sections and it is probably true to say the fewer the better. Too many can lead to confusion. Starting fresh sequences is a habit which is apt to grow—and it is always difficult to draw clear boundary lines, so that each new sequence provides an alternative place to look. In one sequence a file can only be in one place, with ten sequences it can be in ten places.

CHAPTER SIX

Subject Subdivision

One of the chief variable factors displayed between the different press cuttings collections whose practice forms the basis of this chapter is the degree of subdivision of main headings or, looking at the question from another point of view, what subjects are regarded as main headings.

There is a case for standardization of British subject headings on the lines of the American *Sears List.** Nothing like that exists in this country at the present time and, until it does, news libraries will continue to show marked divergencies of terminology and subject breakdown, to the confusion of staff transferring from one library to another.

To start with a sweeping generalization, let us say that too many subdivisions and divisions of subdivisions are inefficient. An ideal hierarchy of no more than two or three should be arrived at. If there appears need for more it should be considered whether or not new main headings are required. Complex ranks forming subsections of subdivisions obstruct rather than assist the search for information. A short hierarchy depends on fairly specific parent headings.

Not every main heading is necessarily subdivided, of course. Most subject arrangements show, in the same sequence, a simple individual heading such as WALKING STICKS followed by a big subject like WATER SUPPLIES which will be divided extensively. Both are main headings. In the case of WALKING STICKS, the subject is more easily found there than if it were buried under some superior heading.

* *Sears List of Subject Headings*, 8th ed., New York, 1959.

The degree of subdivision depends on three factors: the size of the collection, the use made of the library, and the way in which the subject is written about.

The quantity of material to be dealt with is a paramount factor since there is no point in subdividing a file with only half a dozen cuttings in it. The Suez Canal before the 1956 crisis in most libraries was only a single rather dusty folder. Cyprus, until recently, merited only the simplest breakdown, but the position has drastically altered since the island attracted world attention as a trouble spot.

As we have already seen, since it is not dealing with such large quantities of material, the small library can almost avoid subdivision altogether by using only one form of heading in one sequence, e.g.:

DOCK WORKERS	COAST EROSION
DOCTORS	COAST GUARDS
DODECANESE ISLANDS	COCKFIGHTING
DOGS	COCOA
DOLLS	COCOS ISLANDS
DONKEYS	COFFEE
DRINK	COINAGE
DRUGS	COPPER

Everything goes under the most specific heading that will contain it, irrespective of associated subjects. In its extreme form this puts ships direct under their names (e.g. *Queen Mary* under Q), Windows at W, Ospreys at O, Swans at S. The system has a particular advantage in one-man libraries because the collection can be effectively consulted in the absence of the librarian and new readers can quickly grasp the principles. Full references are essential, however, and the system is somewhat wasteful of space since, theoretically, every type of bird needs a separate folder. Before long, as the collection begins to grow, it may be found necessary to group all ships and all birds together and an element of subdivision creeps in.

Once the pure arrangement of single alphabetical headings, unsubdivided, in one sequence, is departed from, a host of problems rush in. Most of them arise in the larger collections. Obviously, the larger the amount of material the more subdivisions required, but not necessarily more *stages* of subdivision.

Certain large libraries and a few small ones use the opposite approach to the 'straight out' method and divide the subject coverage of the collection first into a relatively small number of vast generic classes. Thus we may find:

AGRICULTURE, FOOD, AND FISHERIES

ARTS AND RECREATION
(including Architecture, Gambling, Music, Sport, etc.)

COMMODITIES
(including Products of all kinds)

COMMUNICATIONS AND MASS MEDIA
(including Advertising, Broadcasting, Press and Television, etc.)

HEALTH
(including Doctors, Diseases, Hospitals, Medicines, Mental Health, Public Health, etc.)

INDUSTRIES
(including Electricity, Engineering, Gas, Machine Tools, etc.)

The generic main heading method can, if not strictly controlled, lead to extreme examples of subdivision which hinder access to subjects and do not otherwise serve much useful purpose. To demonstrate with one of the classes above, we may reach this position:

HEALTH
  Hospitals
    Labour
      Nursing staff
        Wages

which is a long road to the simple subject of pay for nurses.

Furthermore, the classes tend to be unchangeable; subheadings are added as necessary, but only rarely is a new main class created. Thus all subjects must be squeezed into the existing main categories and when a new topic arises the instinctive action is to place it under the main heading that most neatly fits it. If none quite fits it still must go under the nearest, for the creation of a new generic class is a major decision. A proper caution in creating new main classes is to be commended but, equally, too rigid an approach to the ever-changing aspects of the day's news leads to some odd subject placings.

Any library using generic classes and not limited in scope to distinct fields is tempted to establish a Generalia or Miscellaneous class. Once this exists the problem of deciding into what class borderline subjects should go becomes accentuated. It is not greatly alleviated by allowing those specific topics not fitted into a main generic class to be scattered throughout the alphabet 'straight out', for one then has an awkward mixture of generic class and direct headings which gets the worst of both worlds.

It is sometimes argued in favour of the generic class system that it is helpful in the biggest libraries on purely physical grounds. Such grouping saves the feet, making it less frequently necessary to walk from one end of the library to another, and perhaps climb ladders in search of associated material. Further, the method makes staff subject specialization easier. Elsewhere, libraries serving research workers who individually concentrate on such main groupings may find that their users prefer main classes since most of their material is thereby stored in the same physical area.

It is interesting to see, as a contrast, that the B.B.C. News Library, with few cuttings on the Beatles pop singers, has simply

MUSIC
    Pop Groups
        Beatles

The *Daily Mirror*, with immense coverage and using the generic class ENTERTAINMENT, has

ENTERTAINMENT
  Music
    Singing
      Popular
        Beatles
        Searchers

The best arrangement for the majority of libraries is probably somewhere between a straight out series of specific headings and the large generic class approach. This gives most specific topics direct main headings, but also subdivides where necessary.

The approach works well enough with subjects lending themselves naturally to subdivision, for example,

DANCING	or	WEATHER
Ballet		Fog
Ballroom		Frost
Folk		Rainfall
Twist		Snow
etc.		Sunshine
		Wind
		etc.

Not all subjects allow such tidy subdivision, however, and with many topics it is an open question whether subdivision or main heading is most useful. To give two very simple examples, we can have

DISEASES	and	METALS
Arthritis		Aluminium
Bronchitis		Brass
Cancer		Copper

or we can have a generalized heading to contain disease or metals broadly discussed and give equal main headings to kinds of disease and metals, e.g.

ALUMINIUM, ARTHRITIS, BRASS, BRONCHITIS, CANCER, COPPER, DISEASES (GENERAL).

The grouping of such topics as in the first example should not be taken too far, or it may lead to inconsistencies and the obscuring of important subjects. For example, if metals are grouped A–Z by name under METALS, what about minerals, such as Salt? And what do you do about vegetable products like Wood or Rubber?

If in doubt, file straight out, is a reliable guide.

A use factor to bear in mind here is that for most new libraries the subject heading is there simply to provide a means of locating cuttings. In a news library the inquirer seeking material on Cancer is not usually concerned with other diseases, and there is thus no special advantage in bringing all diseases together. The direct heading CANCER is simple in use, allows fewer stages of subdivision, and gives direct access to subjects and easier finding.

We saw the same point earlier in this chapter when dealing with pay for nurses. Instead of subdividing under HOSPITALS or HEALTH the direct heading is simpler, e.g.:

NURSES
- Conditions
- Training
- Uniform
- Wages
- Working hours.

In the news library inquiries tend to be specific, and an inquirer wanting nursing pay is not at that time interested in hospitals or even in nurses' uniforms.

It is nevertheless true that a library concerned with economic and industrial matters may wish to bring all metals together. Similarly, a library serving a research worker closely concerned with health affairs may require all diseases under the same heading. If the main user demand requires the subject NURSES in association with hospital matters, this must be allowed for.

Occasionally, the closer association of like subjects may assist inquirers by calling attention to associated material near by.

Let us now go on to consider a further teasing question where extensive subdivisions are in use. Is it wise to attempt a limited amount of classification within a lengthy list of subheadings? For example, which is better?

EDUCATION	or EDUCATION
Adult	Adult
Evening classes	Evening classes
Grammar schools	Workers' Educ. Assn.
Public schools	Secondary
Secondary—general	Grammar schools
Secondary modern schools	Public schools
Workers' Educational Association	Secondary modern schools

The right hand example, a partially classified arrangement tidily dividing each branch of education into its parts before going on to the next, is more logical. But since, as we have seen, inquirers are not usually concerned with related subjects, it is not especially helpful. And from the point of view of the arrangement as a finding device the extra subdivision actually gets in the way. If you are looking for grammar schools EDUCATION: GRAMMAR SCHOOLS is simple. With the classified method one has to stop and consider grammar schools as part of secondary education before the topic can be found. It is partly a question of size. Where the sequence is very lengthy, as the full breakdown of educational subdivisions is, a case can be made out for not separating Workers' Educational Association from Adult Education at the other end of the alphabet.

In any event, the greatest care is necessary when planning new subdivisions to ensure that they do not overlap something already in existence.

It is a matter of some interest to note the principles of subject subdivision preferred by existing libraries. Some of them are not, in fact, satisfied that their system is the best, but where it was set up many years ago the daunting task of changing it is hardly worth the gain. The straight out system of specific direct headings is favoured by *The Guardian*, The *London Evening News*, and the B.B.C. News Library among others. The Labour Party library (a small one) and the *Financial Times* (a big one) both use the generic class method. (Both are somewhat specialized, of course.) The *Daily Mirror*, one of the biggest of all, uses a combination of both, as does the Reuter Library. The *Daily Mail* library, a very long-standing one, uses generic headings.

In planning subdivision the third factor mentioned at the beginning of this chapter is sometimes paramount, i.e. the way in which the subject is written about. In the confused politics of Malaysia, for example, British foreign policy, internal politics, minority questions, and military operations are commonly written about all in the same news item. The same is true of any brand new major topic when it first appears: the Central African Federation question springs to mind, and the flood disaster at Lynmouth. The proper subdivisions only become apparent as the topic clarifies. (This is particularly noticeable in the field of under-developed countries). To try to impose arbitrary divisions too early only creates problems and, for a while at least, chronological division is the only method. With any topic, a subject file which grows too bulky and does not lend itself to subject division can always be divided in this way.

In a strictly pragmatic system like that of a heavily-used press cuttings collection, theoretical breakdowns of a subject into its component divisions are valueless. The subdivisions should be dictated strictly according to the subject coverage of the material to be filed—in other words, according to the way in which the subject is written about. It is no use dividing Music into Dramatic, Vocal, Instrumental, for example, when it is written about as Opera, Choirs, Orchestras, Jazz, Pop, etc.

As a final word on this vital question of subject classification, it should be emphasized that nothing about it is permanent. The essential characteristic of a lively collection is flexibility. Alphabetical arrangement allows infinite new headings at any point in the sequence. Not only should new ones be created as necessary (after proper checking to ensure that they do not already exist in some other form) but old ones can be closed. Subjects which change in emphasis can be brought into line with the new view of them. The classic example is a wages issue which develops into a strike. It is necessary to draw a clear line, filing wages issues under wages until direct industrial action is taken, when it moves from

ENGINEERING Wages	into	ENGINEERING Strikes

The problem in this instance is neatly overcome in *The Times* library by using the term DISPUTES for all labour difficulties.

Sometimes a whole new offshoot can be taken from the main stem and placed elsewhere. A good example of this was 'Rachmanism' which grew out of the Profumo Affair and belonged, after a while, in HOUSING or RACE RELATIONS. Similarly, the 'Great Train Robbery' case in Buckinghamshire in 1963 suddenly shifted in interest to the sinking of the yacht *Christine* which was thought to be associated with the thieves. The wrecking of the *Christine* would normally go in SHIPPING: ACCIDENTS or a similar heading, but special steps have to be taken to link the two events.

It may be said as a final footnote to the question of subject subdivision that one piece of knowledge is essential to success. Successfully to subdivide a heading demands that the subject be *understood* by the classifier. It is too much to expect a thorough knowledge, but the main issues and the relevance and relative importance of the component parts must be clearly in the classifier's mind before a useful breakdown can be achieved.

Some examples from the subject headings sequence of existing libraries may be of interest:

The Reuter Library

(direct headings)

CASTAWAYS
CAVES
CELTS
CENSORSHIP
CENTENARIANS
CHAIN LETTERS
CHEMICAL WARFARE
CIVIL DEFENCE
CLOCKS
CLOWNS
COINCIDENCES
COINS

Labour Party

(generic heading)

LAW AND ORDER
- Censorship
- Civil Rights
- Copyright
  - Patents
  - Trade marks
- Coroners
- International Law
- Judges
- Juries
- Justices of the Peace
- Legal Aid
- Libel
  - etc.

B.B.C.

(direct headings)

LACE TRADE
LADDERS
LAMPREYS
LAMP TRADE
LANCASTER, DUCHY OF
LAND
- General
- Nationalisation
- Reclamation

LANGUAGES
- Arabic
- Basic English
- Esperanto
- etc.

LAUGHTER
LAUNDRIES
LAVENDER

CHAPTER SEVEN

Places and People

(i) PLACES

IT is essential to have clearly in mind from the start the relative prominence to be given to place and subject division in the arrangement. The guiding principle to have in mind is that bias towards place usually makes for easier finding: bias towards subject is better classification.

The place and subject question is clearly dealt with in book classification schemes, such as the Dewey Decimal Classification. Place division as a primary heading scarcely exists in Dewey, and everything goes first under subject, using generic headings. For example, Politics or History are large classes subdivided by country. In the press cuttings collection of a news library this will not do. The emphasis is such that a major part of the news of foreign origin is expected to be found primarily under country.

Home News

Although there are wide differences in practice when dealing with home news, a majority of London newspaper libraries place the major emphasis on subject approach. Thus regional aspects of British subjects are mainly filed with the subject, not the locality. For example, although Birmingham may be divided into

BIRMINGHAM

City Council	Parks
Colour question	Statues
Hotels	Traffic problem
Housing	etc.

many libraries would treat all these except the first as a contribution to the general subject and file under the appropriate subject heading. The colour question in Birmingham may not, indeed, get a separate heading but go in some special aspect of race relations in the library without attempting to isolate the issue in Birmingham.

Similarly, HOUSING is a national issue and Birmingham aspects of it may be more usefully filed under their subjects:

HOUSING
  Absentee Landlords
  Rents
  Slum Clearance

and so forth, than grouped at HOUSING: BIRMINGHAM, or BIRMINGHAM: HOUSING.

The disadvantage of this subject arrangement, of course, is that the library is in danger of defeat if asked for all material on housing in Birmingham. Further, if the request is for a specific cutting on absentee landlords in Birmingham it is a good deal slower in retrieval when filed with the big national question of absentee landlords than if grouped under Birmingham.

For this reason it is practicable to operate the opposite rule if desired, placing national aspects of a topic under the subject but local applications under the locality. It is a matter for decision in the library concerned, bearing in mind the likely demand. We should be clear, however, that it is not possible to be absolutely consistent in application. A typhoid epidemic in Aberdeen, for example, is obviously better with TYPHOID than with ABERDEEN.

A word of warning here. If it is decided to group local issues of national problems under localities, it is necessary also to treat London, i.e. the capital, as a locality. Too often, events taking place in the capital tend to be regarded as national. For example, colour riots in Nottingham go in NOTTINGHAM. Colour riots in Notting Hill, London, should by the same token go under

LONDON. What is really not advisable is to attempt both, e.g.:

HOUSING
- Absentee Landlords
- Birmingham
- Rents
- Slum clearance
- Southampton

A glorious example of cross division. No one would know where to file Absentee Landlords in Birmingham. A way out of this, justified where sufficient detail is required, is the geographical subdivision of subdivisions, e.g.:

COLOUR QUESTION
- Mixed marriages
- Public houses
- Riots and disturbances
  - Birmingham
  - London
  - Nottingham
- Views and statements

or

HOUSING
- Rents
  - Birmingham
  - London
  - Manchester

Another but strictly limited alternative is filing in duplicate, dealt with in Chapter Eight.

The exception noted earlier relates to the CITY COUNCIL or LOCAL GOVERNMENT sub-heading, where the subject matter often tends to be strictly local without much application to national issues. Such material is thus more useful subdivided by place. In response to this some libraries have created a Municipal, Topographical, and Historical sequence (known as MTH or some variant) wherein is filed all local material not more useful elsewhere. Alternatively, as we have already seen, British places form a separate sequence, sometimes included under Great Britain alongside foreign countries.

Thus, we might have

BIRMINGHAM

City Council
Development Schemes
General articles
History
Town Hall
University
etc.

A case can be made out for taking more out of Birmingham if desired, thus

TOWN PLANNING

Bath
Birmingham
Bristol

and

UNIVERSITIES

Birmingham
Cambridge
Manchester
Sussex
etc.

This works well enough with the above two subjects which lend themselves naturally to geographical subdivision but, as we have seen, it is less satisfactory when a clear choice has to be made between subdividing geographically or by subject subdivisions. It is a matter for decision on the spot, applying the rule of filing where it is most useful. In any case, it is essential to have a record under the Birmingham heading of 'Here' and 'Away' material, thus giving a sporting chance of producing 'everything on Birmingham' if required.

Where British place names appear in alphabetical sequence they are probably best arranged directly under the specific name followed by the county, thus giving quick access. Some libraries prefer an arrangement by counties and county boroughs, for the sufficient reason that their provincial correspondents are organized in this way.

The treatment of English provincial matter is taken a stage further by news libraries in the provinces handling material relating to their own locality. It is the function of a provincial library to gather local material and this is usually given special treatment over cuttings relating to affairs outside the circulation area. Thus a local collection is built up.

Since they are dominant, local affairs may be given a library to themselves forming an entirely separate section from other matters, but arranged in parallel lines to it. Under such an arrangement, the place name does not appear in the heading, but will be understood as the supreme subject. That is, WELFARE SERVICES embraces welfare in the area of the local collection only and another heading WELFARE might appear in the general sequence.

On the other hand, where the local collection is not large it may be sufficient to divide it under a place heading in the main sequence. For example, *The Guardian*'s library has all its Manchester material under MANCHESTER in the general sequence, giving the place heading preference for most national topics having specific applications for Manchester.

The weakest method, perhaps, is to employ the home locality subdivision under every main heading, giving preference to filing all local material there irrespective of aspect.

Taking the matter a stage further, the smallest libraries of intensely local coverage can regard locality as supreme subject. For example, a library in Manchester might find the heading BRISTOL: TOWN HALL perfectly adequate. In Bristol, however, it would appear as TOWN HALL.

Wales, Scotland, and Northern Ireland—even the Isle of Man—are usually regarded as place headings for indigenous matters, these taking priority over subject.

Foreign News

Now let us turn to foreign news items. As we have already seen, it is the practice in many libraries to create a separate foreign section arranging everything in it, first by country, and then subdividing within country appropriately by subject. Other libraries include foreign country headings as part of the main subject sequence but each country is subdivided in the same way as if it were part of a separate foreign section.

The order is normally alphabetical by specific country, irrespective of colonial questions or continent, e.g.:

ADEN
ALBANIA
ALGERIA
ANGOLA
AUSTRALIA
etc.

So that Portuguese colonial policy goes under PORTUGAL but specific dependencies such as Angola go with the colony direct. The same was true about news of Algeria before independence. French policies in Algeria were filed with the country: FRANCE: COLONIES takes general items only.

Where library usage tends towards certain territorial groupings, however, the arrangement may be expected to reflect this. Thus at the Royal Institute of International Affairs, African states appear first under AFRICA and Latin American countries go first under that heading because students using the library tend to pursue their studies in those groupings.

Exactly what is filed under country of origin varies widely in different libraries. The simplest rule, which suits a library emphasizing foreign affairs is:

Divide English material first by subject
Divide foreign material first by place then by subject.

Under this principle the main subject headings are 'understood' to be British or International. For example, LABOUR is mainly general labour conditions in Britain and may also include International Labour Organization. French labour is under FRANCE. EDUCATION is necessarily British education: schools in the United States go under UNITED STATES: EDUCATION.

Occasionally, one finds an INTERNATIONAL Section established, taking all topics treated internationally such as I.L.O. above or DISARMAMENT. In most British libraries, however, this is difficult to apply clearly since, for example, abstract discussions of trade unionism can be regarded as of international or British aspect. It is probably wise to employ such a heading with the greatest caution, limiting its use to certain clearly defined subjects such as the United Nations, or it may create more difficulties than it solves.

Full adherence to the foreign news under country of origin principle is fairly simple to follow and gives, in one library:

FRANCE
- Academies
- Accidents
- Advertising
- Aeronautics
- Agriculture
- Aid
- Air Force
- Aliens and Nationality
- Animals
- etc.

A large number of news libraries prefer foreign news treated in this way. The system is easy to apply and use, it provides for a satisfying degree of consistency, and it makes specific items easier to find. Further, it is quickly understood by untrained staff. Undoubtedly, however, as we shall now see, it separates certain items frequently wanted together. You can't have it both ways (but see Chapter Eight: Duplicate Filing).

However strong the bias towards country of origin, it is likely that some major topics should be filed under subject and subdivided geographically rather than filed first under country. For example, most libraries find it useful to break down ATOMIC WEAPONS by country rather than split the subject according to the country concerned. For example:

ATOMIC WEAPONS	not	FRANCE
China		Animals
France		Atomic weapons
Great Britain		Banking
Russia		etc.
United States		

The crux of the problem is which foreign subjects go first under the subject rather than the country of origin?

Let us consider the matter in relation to education—a borderline case.

Where all foreign material goes under country of origin or the country concerned we have

EDUCATION (i.e. *British education*)	and	UNITED STATES
Corporal punishment		Defence
Curriculum		EDUCATION
Examinations		Government
etc.		etc.

This arrangement suits libraries strong on foreign news like those of *The Guardian* or *The Times*.

Others feel, however, as we saw with regional aspects of British subjects, that subject interest takes preference, in many cases, over foreign country.

Thus it is immediately obvious in the above example that whereas English education is treated in some detail, education in the United States is a single heading. So let us break it down:

UNITED STATES
  Education
    Corporal punishment
    Curriculum
    Examinations
    etc.

We now have British and U.S. Corporal Punishment in two places, whereas surely they are likely to be wanted at the same time. An alternative arrangement is to treat education internationally, thus:

EDUCATION
  Corporal Punishment
    Abroad (A–Z by country)
    Great Britain
  Curriculum
    Abroad (A–Z by country)
    Great Britain

It is also necessary in this case to have:

EDUCATION
  General articles
    Belgium
    France
    Germany
    etc.

While education may be regarded as a special type of subject with international implications, the problem applies also to similar topics, like working hours, wages, or religion. In practice what usually happens is that the common sense approach of filing where the subject is most useful is followed. Thus it is quite practicable to file general articles on U.S. education under the country, while specific aspects like corporal punishment go under the subdivision CORPORAL PUNISHMENT of the general EDUCATION heading.

As with our examples of regional aspects of British subjects, preference for subject as opposed to place division suffers from the disadvantage that all material about (say) France cannot conveniently be brought together. This is seldom required, however, although, treating arrangement as a finding device only, the main heading FRANCE provides a good starting point for finding any items of French origin.

A somewhat extreme example of bias towards subject and away from foreign country subdivision might give:

FRANCE	ELSEWHERE
Armed Forces	Accidents
Civil Service	Advertising
Defence	Aeronautics
Finance	Agriculture
Foreign Relations	Aliens
Industry	Archaeology
Trade	Art
	Atomic weapons
	Caves
	Colonies A–Z direct
	Crime
	Customs
	Education
	Labour
	Metals
	Population
	Railways
	Religion

The above arrangement works reasonably well and provides good classification, although it is slower in use than the full breakdown of France we considered earlier. ACCIDENTS, ADVERTISING, AERONAUTICS, AGRICULTURE, ALIENS, ARCHAEOLOGY, etc. are all subdivided geographically where necessary elsewhere in the sequences. In fact, however, few news libraries arrange cuttings in this way. It is fully used, of course, in book classification schemes.

It is likely that the best plan, as usual, is something of a compromise, filing indigenous material under the country of origin and making a decision about subjects like Education which have corresponding aspects in other countries, with the bias towards arrangement by country.

It is interesting to note that *Keesing's Contemporary Archives* (weighted towards foreign affairs), groups the whole of its index entries under country of origin or under supranational bodies. A very few topics, like gold, are given international status and a main heading to themselves. In the *Keesing's* index, all United Kingdom subjects are grouped under UNITED KINGDOM (not recommended for cuttings) as are all French subjects under France. There is thus no 'understood' British emphasis. But *Keesing's*, of course, has a large proportion of export sales.

A group of topics, chiefly natural phenomena, lends itself to subdivision by place. These include:

VOLCANOES
- Italy
- Japan
- South Seas

OIL FIELDS
- Great Britain
- Middle East
- Roumania

EARTHQUAKES
- Chile
- Japan
- Yugoslavia
- etc.

HYDRO-ELECTRIC SCHEMES
- Ghana
- Peru
- Rhodesia
- Scotland

Geographical subdivision works well also with most artistic and scientific subjects.

As we saw when discussing subject breakdown, direct division into a single series of alphabetically arranged subdivisions is generally more helpful than a partially classified arrangement. A single series of headings under country should be the aim. Nevertheless, a case can be made out where the number of divisions is large for some classification. For example, we might usefully have:

FRANCE
- Politics and Government
  - Communists
  - Constitution
  - Elections
  - Fascists
  - Gaullists
  - etc.

or

FRANCE
- Labour
  - Strikes
  - Unions
  - Wages

In the same way it is sometimes convenient to break down foreign relations into:

FRANCE
- Foreign relations
  - Germany
  - Great Britain
  - United States

The alternative is direct headings:

FRANCE
- Germany: Relations
- Great Britain: Relations
- United States: Relations

The Royal Institute of International Affairs imposes a measure of classification as opposed to direct subdivision in its standard subheadings to geographical placings and has, for example:

UNITED STATES	UNITED STATES
Armed Forces	Economic Questions
Air	Agriculture
Army	Customs and Tariffs
Defence	Fisheries
Expenditure	Foodstuffs
Navy	Foreign Trade
etc.	Labour
	etc.

All places and many general subjects require a 'generalities' subheading for items not worth the creation of a specific subheading to themselves, and for articles too general in scope for subdivision. The Reuter Library maintains a separate file for 'Background Articles' under each main subject, containing chronologies, summaries, and similar items which might otherwise be lost from sight beneath later items.

The subdivision PLACES arranged A–Z by place name is useful under foreign countries, thus:

INDIA
  Places
    Bombay
    Delhi
    Hyderabad
    Madras
    etc.

(ii) PEOPLE

The arrangement of cuttings where the person written about is the most important aspect is rather less difficult. First, however, let us consider what is filed under the biographical heading.

Personalities are of enormous importance for news reference work and for many other press cuttings collections also. But every personality is connected in the public mind with the subject with which he is associated, and the two are often written about in the same piece. In general, it is a good rule to place in the biographical files only cuttings providing additional personal data. A man's subject is filed with the subject.

Thus Donald Campbell's motoring records go with motor racing. The file on King Baudouin of the Belgians will contain personal details—marriage, children, etc.—but the Monarchy question in Belgium is filed under BELGIUM. This is even more true of the infamous—Fuchs, Vassall, Lee Oswald, whose personal files are likely to be slender indeed compared with the espionage and assassination files with which they are associated. References and a limited amount of duplicate filing are, of course, essential.

The contrary view is sometimes put forward in favour of filing the main topic with the personality concerned. It is pointed out that with certain difficult forms of inquiry the only common factor is a personal name, and by filing here the library can often answer an inquiry more easily than by seeking it under fine divisions of a subject or, worse, within a mass of material, unsubdivided, on some big subject. This does not seem an entirely satisfactory way out, except in very exceptional circumstances, and may lead to heavy overlapping and duplication.

A few of the most prominent people in public life (alive or dead) are so extensively written about as to require subdivided personal files. This is easy in the case of the dead. Living people are more awkward since their activities change direction and no set of headings can stay constant for long. The *Daily Mirror* file on the Duke of Edinburgh illustrates what can be done. The full series of subdivisions in use is too long to reproduce here and the following is a selection:

EDINBURGH, Philip, *Duke of*

Armistice Day
Birthdays
British Isles Visits
Broadcasts and Television
Cadets
Christenings
Clothing
Dinners, Luncheons, and Receptions
Exhibitions and Shows
Ex-servicemen
Freedoms of Cities
Future Engagements
Guards
Hair
Handwriting
Health
Honours, Ranks, Titles, Decorations, etc.
Household,
etc.

Speeches are usually filed away from biography, but Wills may be filed here or sub-divided A–Z under WILLS. The heading APHORISMS may be included under biography where appropriate, and is a useful aid to feature writers.

The simplest order by which to file biography is alphabetically by the form of name in common use, without regard for nationality, rank, or period. Once the collection grows to any size, however, this arrangement is not as simple as it sounds.

As we have already seen, it is the practice in some libraries, (i.e. the Press Association), to devote a separate sequence to dead biography, transferring files from a living to a dead sequence on the publication of obituary notices. Two chief advantages accrue from this: there is no possibility of mistaking a living peer (say) for his dead father, and there is a certain saving of space. Since the dead sequence is less used it can be packed tighter and the files themselves subjected to heavy weeding.

Whether or not this separation is carried out, the biographical section is, of course, the place for the historic dead and for personal centenary and other celebrations—for example, the Shakespeare Quatercentenary under Shakespeare, and Shakespearean authorship controversies here in preference to some literary heading.

Some libraries with large foreign collections prefer to arrange biography first by country and then alphabetically by name. This has certain advantages with difficult foreign names when it is unclear what part of the name should determine the file's position in the alphabetical sequence. African names (the ONI OF IFE) and those certain countries in South East Asia bedevil easy finding in this respect. Strict filing according to the usage of the country concerned does not always solve the question since the correct usage may not always be known among library inquirers. Provided there are not too many names, grouping under country of origin (or association) has its uses. It is also helpful in the finding of names mis-spelt, or alternatively spelt, as with transliteration from the Cyrillic or other non-Roman alphabets. For example, the name of the former President of the Soviet Presidium is variously spelt in British newspapers as Khrushchev, Kruschev, Krushchev, Khruschev, and Krushchov, to mention only some of the permutations.

On the other hand, filing under nationality is not as direct and fast in retrieval as a single alphabetical sequence and falls down over the placing of certain international personalities (Aga Khan, T. S. Eliot, Charlie Chaplin).

An occasional but not altogether satisfactory compromise takes the form of grouping biographical files in one sequence of surnames with the exception of certain African and Oriental countries where the form of name makes the basic surname arrangement uncertain in operation. Within these country headings forming exceptions, biographical headings are arranged according to national usage. Clear indication of which countries form the exception is, of course, essential or the compromise may prove a snare.

On balance, a direct alphabetical series of names in one sequence has fewest disadvantages. The problems of what part of name to file under are dealt with in Chapter Ten.

While it is generally agreed that alphabetically by name is the right basic approach to biography there is one form of inquiry it does not satisfy. What is to be done when the library is asked to produce all its files on bare-fisted boxers, Indian princes, or other groups of people linked by some special characteristic?

This requires subject arrangement of biography, which is suggested in some book classification schemes. Whatever its merits for books, to attempt to arrange biographical cuttings by subjects, as Film Stars A–Z, Racing Drivers A–Z, British Politicians A–Z, is simply not workable, because many personalities are unclassifiable and some are concerned with more than one activity.

Usually, the subject file or reference books must first provide the names, some of which can then be gathered from the biographical section. *The Guardian* library provides classified indexes by subject and by nationality to its advance obituary section and the idea might usefully be extended to biographical sections elsewhere.

The general comment may be made that it is not good classification to shape a system of arrangement to meet the exceptional inquiry. Day-to-day practical value is the criterion and one cannot always legislate for off-beat inquiries.

CHAPTER EIGHT

Duplicate Filing

MANY of the problems to which solutions have been offered in the foregoing chapters would have been eased a good deal by filing in two places at the same time. To a limited degree, this takes place in practice; but because it was necessary to consider subject allocation in its purest form this course has been deliberately ignored until now.

In fact, since two press cuttings take up very little more space than one, all press libraries rely on multi-copies at times to help them provide full coverage. For the library of a newspaper this is no problem with the home paper, for additional copies (usually 'spoils') cost nothing. (As we have seen, the *Daily Telegraph* library cuts up to 70 copies of the home paper a day.) Newspapers which have to be paid for, however, are a different matter and the cost factor is an important one in keeping down the number of duplicates. It does not follow, however, that duplicates must all be taken from the same newspaper. If the item is not an exclusive it will be found in several newspapers, perhaps treated differently but each one good enough as a supplementary source of reference.

Used wrongly, duplicate filing is the refuge of the woolly minded and soon chokes the files with inappropriate material. Used intelligently, however, a limited number of extra copies distributed in the right files can save the day time and again. Indeed, in some cases, duplication is essential to ensure complete files.

The principle is: use duplicates on brief non-recurring issues where there is a genuine duality of interest. Do not file complete subjects in duplicate; these are matters for decision and reference from alternatives.

The correct use of duplicate copies depends on the needs of the library. Some examples will help.

Their use is fully justified, for instance, over items with both biographical and subject interest. New appointments are among the chief of these. The chairman of a Royal Commission is announced: clearly, to obtain comprehensive record a cutting goes with the Royal Commission subject (Gambling, the Press) and another with the chairman's biographical file. Scientists and their inventions are a similar case and there are hundreds of others.

The principle can be repeated with events concerning more than one person, for example when two prominent persons are married or divorced. Continuing topics, however (for example, the Craig–Bentley murder trial) require filing once only, with a reference from the alternative heading.

Duplicates are required also for multi-subject items: such as conferences discussing a variety of topics, like the British Association annual conference when several dozen important scientific papers are presented. A similar example is the annual meeting (say a Chamber of Commerce) which produces an outstanding topic of discussion. The main press story may be of a proposed trade fair, but the library will wish to record the annual meeting as such and require an additional copy with Chamber of Commerce.

It is not difficult to think of many more examples. Policy statements of political parties under specific topics as well as the party; speeches with the subject as well as at SPEECHES A–Z by author; and, as we have seen, both place and subject filing, such as rents in Birmingham with BIRMINGHAM: HOUSING as well as with HOUSING: RENTS, and so on.

This type of multi-filing continued over a period has its dangers however. For example, take a controversial issue from today's paper 'Do sparrows spread fowl pest?' Provided this story appears once only, no harm is done by filing a cutting with bird nuisance as well as with poultry diseases. It is wrong, however, to continue indefinitely to file two parallel sets of cuttings on the topic. It is unlikely ever to be done consistently and thus neither file will be complete. Moreover, the library can seldom spare the room for so lavish an approach. A decision must be taken on the best placing and a slip reference (see Chapter Eleven) placed in the alternative.

The same may be said of reports of an electricians' strike at London Airport by a trade union over a demarcation dispute. It is surely wrong to try to file at Airports, Electrical Industry, Trade Unions, Inter-Union disputes and every other possible aspect. A decision should be taken over the best place and references made from the others.

Duplicates should be used fully and consistently or not at all. An inquirer finding one or two cuttings in a file is entitled to expect that those represent the whole subject. He can be severely misled if, in fact, these two items are placed there as a kind of insurance, with the main body of the material elsewhere. It is vital to be consistent and take a clear line on the classification of big issues.

It must be said, however, that in practice a number of libraries choose the opposite course to the one here advocated, and regularly file big subjects in duplicate or triplicate at different headings. For example, we find trade between two foreign countries, filed under both or, perhaps, cuttings on the Bristol Old Vic Theatre under THEATRES (Subject) and under BRISTOL (Place). In spite of the lengthy discussion we gave to the correct placing in the last chapter some libraries solve the problem of race riots in Nottingham by placing it under both headings. The reason lies in the intense pressure to provide instant service and, to some extent, the use of untrained staff. It is also claimed as an insurance against the loss of cuttings which would otherwise be unique and irreplaceable.

CHAPTER NINE

Some Special Problems

THOSE who have read thus far will have no illusions about the difficulties of subject classification. Each topic carries its own problems and no rule of thumb will solve all of them. The only rule which can be applied has already been referred to:

> Divide material according to the natural development of the subject and according to the likely demand to be made of the library.

Some subjects which are in constant demand are represented in every news library. Notes on the treatment of these may be helpful.

(a) *Politics and Parliament*

The politics of countries overseas should be filed with the country. United Kingdom politics and political policies are generally filed under the name of the party, e.g. LABOUR PARTY POLICY. The simple heading POLITICS is far too general to contain anything useful and should be limited to the main class heading for libraries using the generic class approach.

Parliamentary debates relating to specific subjects are filed with the subject. Domestic parliamentary news may be divided into Lords, Commons, Speaker, etc., under the general heading PARLIAMENT. These files are intended to hold only historical and procedural matters (plus such lighter questions as pay, kitchens, press gallery, accommodation) and not the debates. Bills and Acts of Parliament go with the subject.

PLATE I The openly-planned *Times* Intelligence Department with newspaper slopes and press-cuttings cabinets on the right, bound volumes of cuttings on left and power-operated compact shelving units storing biography and pamphlets in the background. *Photo: D. Morris & Co.*

PLATE II The *Daily Mirror* library stores cuttings in cabinets of shallow drawers banked to eight feet high. Thus a very large amount of material can be retained in a relatively small floor area at some sacrifice to convenience of access. *Photo: Daily Mirror*

LATE III The *New York Daily News* editorial library, with filing cabinets arranged at right angles
› the windows and the work area separate but adjacent to the cuttings. *New York Daily News*

LATE IV A section of the library of the *Philadelphia Inquirer* showing the book collection, with
ve-drawer cuttings cabinets in the foreground.

PLATE V At the Reuter library an assistant helps an editorial writer with information from the lateral files of news messages. Note the convenience of the projecting shelf.

PLATE VI The Press Association library employs a number of five-drawer quarto filing cabinets for press cuttings and P.A. copy, enabling 25% more material to be stored in the same floor space as normal four-drawer cabinets. A stool is needed to reach the transfer cases on top of the vertical files. *P.A.-*

PLATE VII Part of *The Guardian* annual index, which is prepared on cards, with a new series of drawers added each year. *Guardian photo*

PLATE VIII The job of indexing *The Guardian* is divided between two indexers, typing entries direct on to cards with the newspaper supported on a stand behind the typewriter. *Guardian photo*

PLATE IX Classifying cuttings at the *Daily Telegraph*. Less frequently-used newspapers are kept in wide drawers beneath the reading slopes in the background. *Photo: Daily Telegraph*

PLATE X A corner of the *Financial Times* library with work in progress on the current loose-leaf index ledgers. Entries are transferred to cumulative sheaf binders after a year. Note the lateral filing bay for press cuttings and the filing trolley on wheels. *London Press Photos*

ᴄᴇ xɪ The inquiry desk at *The Times*. Cabinets housing press cuttings are shown in the back-
ᴊnd. The deeper drawers contain pamphlet material. *Times photo*

ᴄᴇ xɪɪ Microfilm of *The Times* is stored in a separate room equipped with a viewer and volumes
'he Times Index. The greater part of the back file consultation is done here, and the wear on bound
ımes is correspondingly lighter. *Times photo*

PLATE XIII A general view of the *Daily Mirror* library showing the work area. The cuttings files are out of the picture behind the vertical filing cabinets in the background. *Photo: Daily Mirror*

(b) *Political Issues*

As we have seen, political issues go with the subject. Specific aspects of major issues may go with the precise subject. For example, NATIONALIZATION is a main heading or, perhaps, a subdivision of INDUSTRY; but, nationalization of steel with STEEL, and of water supplies under that heading. Similarly, resale price maintenance is an aspect of economic policy to be filed as a subdivision of PRICES; but, book prices with BOOK TRADE or PUBLISHING, chocolate prices with CONFECTIONERY, and so on. All aspects of a specific industry or commodity are thus kept together.

There is, however, a time factor to be considered. While the subject is white hot and under discussion, the effect of resale price maintenance on all commodities may be required together and provision must be made for this. It is likely also that a library specialising in political theory will require all aspects of nationalization together, just as a library particularly interested in prices (for example, the *Financial Times*) may wish all prices under that heading subdivided by product. It is undesirable to insist on rigid observance of principle. Usage is the primary factor.

(c) *Foreign Relations*

Relations between Great Britain and individual foreign countries are classified with the foreign country. The main heading FOREIGN POLICY or its equivalent is best reserved for general questions (including foreign affairs debates in the House). Indeed, it may not be necessary at all. It is poor practice to create broad 'dustbin headings' like POLITICS, FOREIGN POLICY, or ECONOMICS, which can be used for practically anything, and therefore are useful for nothing.

When two foreign countries or Great Britain and a foreign country are discussing a third country or a specific topic the cuttings are filed with the third country or the subject. (E.g. British–Argentine discussion of the Falkland Islands goes with the FALKLAND ISLANDS. An Iceland–Russia dispute over fishing rights goes in FISHING: INTERNATIONAL WATERS, or equivalent.) When two countries are in dispute over the territory of one of them the cuttings are filed with the country whose territory is under dispute. General relations between two foreign countries go under the first in the alphabet unless there is a good reason for filing elsewhere.

(d) *United Nations*

Debates, reports, and actions on specific topics go with the topic (e.g. U.N. action in the Congo in CONGO). The U.N. files contain constitution, membership, and the U.N. as such. If required, Security Council meetings and plenary sessions can be filed here chronologically under subheadings, e.g. UNITED NATIONS: SECURITY COUNCIL, but some contribution under the subject heading is essential if these files are to be complete. Special U.N. bodies such as the United Nations International Children's Emergency Fund (UNICEF) go with the subject, in this case CHILDREN.

To try to bring all U.N. bodies together under UNITED NATIONS may suit a library with special interest in the organization but, duplicate filing apart, it means robbing the appropriate subject files.

(e) *Europe*

European problems bedevil not only international relations but the classifier attempting to reduce the acres of news on Continental matters to some sort of order. Western European questions can loosely be divided into Political Union, Defence, Economic Union (including trade) and relations with non-European powers among many other issues. Within these broad divisions are a host of associated matters. Each main topic has its quota of supra-national bodies, usually designated by initials (European Economic Co-operation, Western European Union, European Free Trade Area, Council of Europe, and many more).

The usual method of treating these is to file all of them first under the superior head—EUROPE, as follows:

EUROPE, WEST	or	EUROPE, WEST
Common Market		Trade
Council of Europe		Common Market
Western European Union		East–West trade
etc.		etc.

Commonly, the supra-national body forms a subdivision of the subject it represents, keeping the organization heading as far as possible for domestic matters particular to the organization and wider discussions of the subject with the superior heading. For example, European Payments Union may be:

EUROPE, WEST
  Financial Aspects
    European Payments Union

so that E.P.U. specifically goes in the final subdivision while general questions of finance in Europe go with the FINANCIAL ASPECTS subdivision. A certain amount of overlapping is inevitable and, in the smaller libraries, some prefer to group the subject and its organization together without attempting subdivision, e.g.

EUROPE, WEST
  Federation (includes Council of Europe).

Bearing in mind these difficulties it should be considered whether it may not sometimes be better to file as much as possible away from the EUROPE heading, treating its defence, trade matters, etc., internationally, Thus we might have:

TRADE
  European Common Market
  European Free Trade Area

Filing under EUROPE has the effect of isolating European aspects of international subjects from the international aspect. For example, trade between East and West Europe is part of the world issue of East–West trade. It is probably better as:

TRADE	than	EUROPE
East–West		Trade
Europe		East–West Trade

Conversely, the use of the superior heading EUROPE, brings all aspects of Europe together.

The North Atlantic Treaty Organization is not an exclusively European body and is variously filed directly under title or under DEFENCE.

(f) *Military Operations*

Press librarians being concerned in the main with recent events, the collections relating to the last war have been drastically thinned or, tragically, have sometimes disappeared altogether. Very often, in the last war, virtually a separate sequence devoted to aspects of the war was set up. Military operations became a separate main section of the War Library divided into two parallel sequences: the first being OPERATIONS, divided according to the theatre of war, and the other consisting of the various specialist activities: ESPIONAGE, CIVIL DEFENCE, AIR RAIDS, CASUALTIES, plus ARMY, NAVY, AIR FORCE for their service matters not directly connected with battle.

Local wars since 1945 are grouped under the country concerned (KOREA, VIETNAM). Military operations form a separate subdivision. Unfortunately, particularly in the early stages, news is not written in such tidy subdivisions and political and military matters are often written up together. Provided the subject does not grow too unmanageable, chronological arrangement under a broad heading is possible—perhaps the only way. As the subject clarifies it will be necessary to re-arrange under appropriate headings.

(g) *Crime*

To the library of a popular newspaper in particular, crime news is of great importance. The more so because, as we have already noted, newspapers contain virtually the only published crime reports, at any rate for a long period after the case has become known.

The smaller libraries do not, for the most part, collect crime on any scale. Where this is done it is usual to file directly under the name of the offence as a main heading and subdivide chronologically or by a broad grouping of initial letters of defendants' names. (*The Times Index* enters under personal names only, with no reference under type of offence.)

Murder is the crime remaining longest in the public mind. Individual cases are best listed alphabetically by the name of the victim, since this is the first and sometimes the only name known. Unknown victim cases go with the best known title—the name usually given to the case by the newspapers, with references from other forms. For example:

MURDERS
  Brighton Trunk Case
  Moon Murders
  Potters Bar Murder

A card index of references to crime, to murderers, witnesses, etc., is useful to those libraries needing such information. Crime in other countries most usefully goes with the country.

The *Daily Mirror* library has perhaps the best collection of cuttings on crime in this country, where a separate sub-library cuts the subject exhaustively. Crime in the *Daily Mirror* library is arranged alphabetically by the name of the offence. The section begins ABDUCTION, ABORTION, ACID ATTACKS, and goes on through several hundred direct headings to WAGES THEFTS. Headings are subdivided A–Z with subdivisions for well known cases, e.g. ART AND ANTIQUE ROBBERIES: GOYA WELLINGTON

PORTRAIT. Crime in foreign countries appears under the name of the country in a separate sequence, e.g. FRANCE: CRIME: MURDER: DRUMMOND. Comprehensive card indexes and lists are in use for all personal names, not only of defendants and victims, but of judges, witnesses, and counsel. Cases with which barristers and judges are concerned get at least a reference in the personal file (Biographical Section) and perhaps the cuttings as well. Biographical files of habitual criminals are arranged A–Z under CRIMINALS in the same sequence as crimes.

In addition, the *Daily Mirror* produces for internal use an annual 'Murder Book', with alphabetical lists of murders, dates, death sentences, reprieves, comparison tables, and so forth. The Press Association prepares similar lists annually.

(h) *Civil Actions*

These, like crime, are usually grouped under type of case, LIBEL AND SLANDER, TRESPASS, DIVORCE, and subdivided alphabetically by the first letter of the surname of the litigant appearing first in the alphabet, with references from other appropriate names. (As before noted, *The Times Index* uses the personal names of litigants direct.)

(i) *Sport*

Obviously, sport is arranged by the type of sport. A number of popular newspaper libraries give sport a section to itself—almost a separate library, as the *Daily Mirror* does with crime. Basic subdivisions of each sport present few difficulties and include:

CLUBS A–Z
CONTROVERSIES
RECORDS AND STATISTICS
RULES

Sport, as it is written about in newspapers, depends heavily on personalities and a good case can be made out for a separate collection of sporting biography, arranged alphabetically irrespective of sport. This is fairly simple in operation. Efforts to arrange sporting biography under the name of the sport are seldom successful. Some libraries keep sporting biography with the main biography section (the *Daily Mirror*, for example) and this certainly overcomes the difficulty of deciding what is a sportsman (Racing drivers? Lord Lonsdale? Sir Stanley Rous?) Correct arrangement and special care over sport are well repaid since good sporting reference books are few and not all of them fully comprehensive.

(j) *Organizations and Societies*

Most specialist or regional supra-national organizations are filed as subdivisions of the subject (e.g. Food and Agriculture Organization under FOOD). Except for annual general meetings and domestic matters it is not usually possible to separate an organization from the wider discussion of its subject. The two are written about together and often required together. A subdivision for the domestic aspect of the organization may be necessary, e.g.:

HEALTH
World Health Organization

Nevertheless, the straight out system is often used, putting World Council of Churches at W and SEATO direct under SOUTH EAST ASIA TREATY ORGANIZATION, particularly in smaller libraries and those using direct heading arrangement.

The same system may be used for British organizations, putting (say) HOWARD LEAGUE FOR PENAL REFORM under H. There is no doubt, then, where an organization is to be found in the sequence. The system is clumsy, however, when dealing with the hundreds of organizations whose titles begin with the word NATIONAL, or BRITISH.

This is one point in favour of the alternative method, filing under a key word, but the system needs careful handling. Thus we would have:

PENAL REFORM, HOWARD LEAGUE FOR

which may bring the organization close to its subject in the alphabetical sequence.

Best of all, probably, as we saw above for supra-national bodies, is grouping as a subdivision of the subject, e.g.

LAW
  Penal Reform
    Howard League

so that general discussion of penal reform, including Howard League, is filed next to Howard League cuttings.

The B.B.C. News Library uses a combination of both the above, putting some organizations directly under the title and others grouped as subdivisions of the subject.

Subjects with a large number of organizations may find the subheading ORGANIZATIONS useful, arranged loosely A–Z if warranted, e.g.:

EDUCATION
  Organizations A–Z

TRANSPORT
  Organizations A–Z

Here and there one finds ORGANIZATIONS used as a main heading on the ground that some bodies are difficult to classify by subject, e.g. ROYAL INSTITUTION, PEOPLE'S LEAGUE, MORAL RE-ARMAMENT. Rather than bury important organizations under an arbitrary main head, it might seem better to file direct under the title.

Specific business firms and manufacturing companies can be treated in the same ways we have discussed for organizations.

(k) *Trade Unions and Employers' Associations*

These are best filed with the industry on the same principle as other organizations. A prominent heading for TRADE UNIONS in general will also be necessary, but Amalgamated Engineering Union with ENGINEERING INDUSTRY and the P & KTF under PRINTING: TRADE UNIONS. Wage discussions, strikes, and other labour matters in which trade unions take part go with the appropriate subdivision of the industry.

(l) *Labour*

Each library will need such a general subject as a main heading, to contain general material. Specific aspects not related to a single industry may appear as subdivisions of LABOUR or take main headings in their own right, e.g.:

LABOUR	or	LABOUR, GENERAL
Strikes		STRIKES
Trade Unions		WAGES
Wages		WORKING HOURS
Working Hours		

The usual practice is to file wages, strikes, working hours of a particular industry under the industry, as follows:

COAL MINING
- Coalfields A–Z
- Collieries A–Z
- Exports
- Labour
- Mechanization
- Pit Ponies
- Production
- Strikes
- Subsidence
- Trade Unions
- Wages
- Working Hours

At least one library, however, has a tidy arrangement, placing labour questions in all industries together, as follows:

LABOUR

Absenteeism
Agriculture
Aircraft and Airport
Atomic Energy

An element of cross division? What about absenteeism in the aircraft industry? In practice when faced with the cuttings, there is little difficulty provided the scope of each heading is precisely understood.

In some cases, STRIKES, WAGES, etc. may form main headings, e.g.:

STRIKES	WAGES
Coal	Coal
Docks	Docks
Electricity	Electricity

The divorce of these aspects of industries from each other, when they are often written about together, is apparent and the system is not recommended.

(m) *Accidents*

These are best classified by type of accident and arranged under that heading, e.g.:

AIRCRAFT	SHIPPING
Accidents	Accidents

Domestic and unusual accidents present a problem, usually requiring a general heading, ACCIDENTS. This difficulty sometimes leads to the use of the opposite approach, ACCIDENTS: AIRCRAFT; ACCIDENTS: SHIPPING.

(n) *Ships and Aircraft*

Ships of all countries are usually arranged A–Z by name under the superior heading SHIPS irrespective of nationality, which may be difficult to establish.

New aircraft are tricky since they are known by various names —the manufacturer's number, the popular name, and so on. Some libraries therefore subdivide under AIRCRAFT first by the name of the manufacturer—Vickers, Boeing, etc.—and then by name, so that if there is any doubt the relevant material cannot, in any case, be very far apart. If required, foreign aircraft may go first under the country, but the balance of usefulness appears to lean towards A–Z by name without regard for nationality.

Fighting ships and aircraft may conveniently be grouped with civil ones. The headings AIR FORCE and NAVY are usefully restricted to service and strategic matters.

(o) *Speeches*

Speeches are of the greatest importance to news libraries since some of them are long remembered—perhaps owing to the use of some striking phrase—but they are most difficult to trace afterwards. Apart from those made in Parliament, many speeches are recorded nowhere else than in newspapers and accordingly must be cut fully—particularly those made by prominent people.

They are usually cut in duplicate: one copy with the subject and another with SPEECHES arranged A–Z by the name of the person making the speech. A number of libraries prefer to use SPEECHES as a subdivision of the appropriate biographical file. It is sometimes necessary in addition to file the speech with the occasion, for example, speeches made at the Royal Academy annual dinner will be required with the Royal Academy. Similarly, speeches made at a teachers' conference go not only with the particular educational topic under discussion but also at the appropriate teachers' organization. Where of sufficient importance and length a speech report may also be divided between different subjects making it clear on the cutting, who made the speech and where.

The Press Library of the Royal Institute of International Affairs files speeches with the subject but maintains an extensive

Speeches Index arranged on cards under the name of the person making the speech. The card gives the main subject of the speech, the newspaper it was reported in, the date, and where it was filed.

(p) *Religion*

Libraries using the generic heading arrangement will group all aspects of religion under that heading and subdivide by creed, e.g. BUDDHISM, MOHAMMEDANISM (or MOSLEMS), etc. Specific Christian sects are better shown direct and equal with non-Christian religions, e.g. CATHOLIC CHURCH, JEHOVAH'S WITNESSES, etc., rather than as subdivisions of some ponderous heading like CHRISTIANITY.

Elsewhere, ignoring the generic heading RELIGION, the same general procedure is followed, all religious denominations being filed under direct headings. The use of the heading RELIGION in non-generic libraries is to be avoïded since it comes into the 'dustbin' category, embracing everything, referred to under FOREIGN POLICY.

In British libraries Anglican Church affairs may be grouped under the main heading CHURCH OF ENGLAND more or less as follows:

CHURCH OF ENGLAND

- Benefices
- Celebacy
- Clergy
  - Dwellings
  - Irregularities
- Prayer Book
- Sermons
- Services
- Synods and Convocations

Some might prefer CLERGY filed direct and away from CHURCH OF ENGLAND, perhaps treating PRAYER BOOK in the same way.

SOME SPECIAL PROBLEMS

Certain other topics associated with religion are best treated as main headings also, for example, BIBLE, CHRISTENINGS, HYMNS, MISSIONARY ACTIVITIES (A–Z by Denomination) and SUNDAY OBSERVANCE (better than SABBATARIANISM).

Church views on a topic, e.g. Divorce, Birth Control, Colour Bar, go with the subject.

Religious organizations embracing more than one denomination may be treated like secular societies, e.g. BRITISH COUNCIL OF CHURCHES.

Religious matters and churches in a specific country go with the country, e.g.:

INDIA
    Church of South India

CHAPTER TEN

File Headings

THE correct allocation of subject headings is of the greatest importance in a library which depends on an alphabetical system of arrangement. The form of heading, too, is important, because the first word of the title of a subject determines its place in the scheme. Time spent on deciding the best form of heading is never wasted.

Librarians concerned mainly with books have paid a great deal of attention to subject headings and some of the principles they have arrived at can be applied to press cuttings also. Headings for the general collection of newspaper cuttings present unique problems, however, and we have seen already how some of them appear in existing newspaper and broadcasting libraries.

Headings for press cuttings are likely to be more specific or subject to more detailed subdivision than those for books. They must allow frequent adjustment and the insertion of unexpected new angles from time to time. They will also cover new subjects long before these are dealt with in books and the news librarian has to be something of a pioneer and something of a prophet in allocating subject headings to news stories while they are still in the course of development.

While we can suggest certain basic principles, few useful guides exist to contemporary headings. *The Times Index*, published at two monthly intervals, is a good guide, but it has to be remembered that this is an *index* and is more specific than a classification scheme (see next chapter). A similar objection applies to the monthly index of *Keesing's Contemporary Archives* which is also too fine in subdivision for cuttings.

In the daily job of classifying and allocating headings the news librarian is, therefore, very much on his own, with only his common sense and experience to guide him. A few points may be helpful.

Consistency is essential and to ensure that uniformity of heading is followed throughout it is wise to prepare a code of practice which can be kept up-to-date as new precedents are created.

Some degree of standardization of subheadings is helpful so that the library always uses (say) LABOUR as a subdivision not WORKERS, and DISPUTES not STRIKES. As we saw in Chapter Seven, standardization should also be imposed on basic foreign country subdivisions.

For many subjects such general subdivisions as ATTITUDES, COMMENT AND CRITICISM, and IRREGULARITIES are useful. Dramatic forms like DISASTERS or SHIPWRECKS instead of ACCIDENTS, are out of place in the library. Although cotton workers are known as operatives and meat porters as bummarees, for the library they are all simply LABOUR.

It is unwise to be too pedantic about titles, however. The popular form is perfectly all right provided it is clear and specific. Everyday usage is the thing to aim at. Terms like MODS, BEATNIKS, POP ART, in quotes if necessary, helpfully delineate certain topical news items. Likewise, if the world calls it BINGO, so should the library and not continue stuffily with a heading for HOUSEY HOUSEY.

For similar reasons, when there is a choice between the popular or technical form of name the most popular should usually be chosen, e.g. BELL RINGING not CAMPANOLOGY, POISONS not TOXICOLOGY.

The headings should also be quite specific, e.g. COAL MINING: not MINING. They must fit the subject exactly and not allow misinterpretation. For this reason the unqualified heading DIVING is bad; it should appear as two or possibly three subjects, PEARL DIVING, SUBMARINE DIVING and, possibly, SWIMMING AND DIVING.

It is necessary that headings be quite clear and not in any way ambiguous or they will from time to time attract items filed in error. Some titles need qualification, e.g. SEALS (ANIMALS) prevents the filing there of items concerning documentary seals. Similarly DRUGS (NARCOTICS) distinguishes these from medicines. Overlapping headings may occasionally be qualified in the negative, e.g. MINING (not COAL MINING).

Where there is a choice between singular and plural forms the plural should be chosen, e.g.:

COLORADO BEETLES	not	COLORADO BEETLE
MINORITIES	not	MINORITY

Abbreviated forms and sequences of initial letters used in headings (W.V.S., R.A.F., St Lawrence) should be arranged as if spelt in full. Figures, if standing alone among letters, should be spelt out (1922 Committee as Nineteen Twenty-Two Committee). A series of figures should be arranged in numerical order, e.g.:

GLOUCESTERSHIRE REGIMENT

1st battalion
2nd battalion
3rd battalion, etc.

Dates are best in inverse chronological order:

OLYMPIC GAMES 1964
1960
1956

Some of the previous examples we have referred to are adjectival headings: names like FIRE INSURANCE, RIVER POLLUTION, ROAD SAFETY, DIPLOMATIC IMMUNITY, ATOMIC ENERGY. The rule is to file such names under the first word of the title unless some other form is decidedly more significant or more generally useful. Some of the foregoing may be inverted if it is desired to bring all types of insurance together or all types of pollution, e.g.:

INSURANCE, FIRE	POLLUTION, ATMOSPHERIC
INSURANCE, LIFE	POLLUTION, RIVER
INSURANCE, WEATHER	

It is likely, however, that where such forms are required together they are best shown as sub-divisions of the main heading:

INSURANCE	POLLUTION
Fire Insurance	Of the atmosphere
Life Insurance	Of rivers
Weather Insurance	

Certainly there is no case at all for pointless inversions such as ENERGY, ATOMIC or IMMUNITY, DIPLOMATIC. It is interesting to note, however, that *The Times Index* has

LIVING, cost of
LIVING, standard of

to bring together these two similar items.

Adjectival forms of main heading such as LEGAL or MEDICAL as are occasionally found serve little purpose when there is a perfectly good noun available.

In the case of compound place names the principle is that proper names of localities should be listed in full and filed under the first word of the title, e.g.:

BRITISH GUIANA under B
SOUTH AFRICA under S
NORTH SHIELDS under N

Compound names loosely describing regions may be inverted provided the inversion serves some useful purpose so that many libraries have:

GERMANY, East	EUROPE, East
GERMANY, West	EUROPE, West

English localities are filed under the best known form of name, e.g.:

YARMOUTH	not	GREAT YARMOUTH
HULL	not	KINGSTON UPON HULL

Pedantry is out of place in the news library.

The filing and allocation of personal names is not too difficult where English usage is concerned. They are filed under surname, of course, and certain concessions are usually made to obtain simplicity of filing. Thus all names beginning with Mc or Mac are filed as if spelt Mac. In the interest of drawing the line somewhere it is probably unwise to go further and file all CLARKES and CLARKS as if spelt CLARK, and to group together THOMPSONS and THOMSONS. It should be said, however, that many newspaper libraries which are plagued with hurried requests for biographical cuttings on names of which the true spelling is in doubt or wrong, find such an arrangement useful.

St is usually filed as if spelt in full. Decisions over the treatment of prefixes and hyphenated forms are mainly important to ensure consistency rather than because of some intrinsic merit. English names with prefixes are usually filed under the prefix, e.g. St John under S, De la Mare under D. Prefixes in foreign names are too common for this to be effective and it is usual to ignore them, e.g. Von Cramm under C, de Lesseps under L.

With compound names go always for the simplest form, filing under the second part since there is often confusion as to whether an apparent compound is one of the Christian names. (But LLOYD GEORGE under L because this usage is nowadays universal.)

When confronted with similar or the same forms of name, the final description of a person as *poet, politician, socialist politician,* etc., is necessary. For example:

CONNELL, John, *writer and critic*
CONNELL, John, *anti-noise campaigner*

In cases of doubt about the choice of name to be used for authors, actors, and others using pseudonyms, and of any other person capable of being referred to by more than one form of name, the name by which he is most commonly known should be chosen. It does not help anybody to file Marilyn Monroe as Norma Mortensen, the name she was born with, or even, at one time, as Mrs Arthur Miller. Similarly, care must be taken to change titles at once, as when Lord Hailsham reverted to Mr Quintin Hogg, and Sir Anthony Eden became Lord Avon, so that personalities in the news appear always under the latest name.

British royalty appears under Christian name or title in the Biographical Sequence, as:

> ELIZABETH, *Queen Mother*
> KENT, Princess Marina, *Dowager Duchess of*

Many news libraries, however, prefer grouping under the superior heading ROYAL FAMILY or equivalent. The heading ROYALTY is divided A–Z by country of origin in the *Daily Mirror* library. All royalty is thus grouped by nationality, including throneless royalty. The method has practical value since such files are often required in groups, e.g. royal wedding guests.

Foreign names, especially non-European names, present some particularly difficult problems. Where the language is unfamiliar and local usage unknown—as is the case frequently with files referring to the politicians of new countries in Africa and the Orient—it is only possible to make a choice and refer from alternatives. As we saw earlier, the unsatisfactory nature of these decisions has led a number of libraries to arrange foreign biography under country of origin so that similar forms of name are brought together.

Very often, English usage is the best guide when no other presents itself, for local usage, even when trouble has been taken to find out about it, is not generally known to library users. Thus, although we are told that in Malayan names the prefix U merely signifies uncle, it is still satisfactory to file U TIN TUT, or U THANT directly under U. It works.

The Reuter Library, with a large collection of foreign biographies, which is added to daily, goes to great trouble to find out the correct form by contacting embassies and other specialists. The proper form chosen, the personality is filed at that heading, in accordance with the *ALA Code** and with references from territorial titles, rank, etc., where necessary. The Reuter collection is effectively controlled by a card index to all files in use. The cards themselves carry biographical notes.

In general the news librarian has to act on his own over the filing of names because he is dealing often with new personalities before they appear in the reference books and he can have few standards to guide him. One of the best, however, is the name index to *Keesing's Contemporary Archives* which provides a good example of alphabetical arrangement by family name, irrespective of country.

Keesing's gives:

ADENIJI-ADELE II, *Oba of Lagos*, with references from LAGOS and ADELE

IFE, ONI OF *see* ADERIMI II

ROBERTO, Holden (also known as Jose Gilmore and Roberto HOLDEN) with appropriate references

THANT, U

URUNDI (later BURUNDI) MWAMI OF *see* MWAMBUTSA IV

It is worth pointing out, however, that the *Keesing's* Name Index is arranged in 4 column pages so that a range of names can be seen at a glance. A row of 50 filing cabinets is a different field in which to find one's way. And in those libraries which allow direct consultation of the files by users without prior reference to the staff the simplest form will always be the favourite.

* *A.L.A. Cataloguing Rules for Author and Title Entries*, American Library Association, 2nd ed., 1949.

(There was more to be said about the basic arrangement of biography in Chapter Seven.)

It should not be necessary to say that it is most unwise to group biographical cuttings of several persons together so that those beginning with the same three letters (BENSON, BENTLEY, BENTON) or with the same initials (CLARKE, A–C, CLARKE, D–F), are filed together. All collections grow and the complexities this faulty approach brings in its train are endless. If a personal cutting is worth keeping it deserves a file to itself.

Turning now to subject headings once more, not all libraries will wish to employ subject headings in full. Time and space can be saved by devising a system of abbreviations which can reduce the form of heading to a minimum while not entirely obscuring its meaning. Each library will arrive at its own favourites, which become the jargon of the staff. A few examples may be helpful. The *Daily Mirror* has:

ESC	Egypt: Suez Canal
FR	Foreign Relations
PPL	Parliamentary Parties: Labour
RGM	Rockets and Guided Missiles
S AND A	Societies and Associations
C AND C	Comment and Criticism

The Reuter Library uses:

ANARCH	Anarchists
ANNIV	Anniversaries
ASSAS	Assassinations
AUCT	Auctions
AV	Aviation

The Royal Institute of International Affairs has EST (Espionage, Sabotage, Treason).

The fullest use of mnemonic abbreviations is made by the *Radio Times* Hulton Picture Library which, although used for illustrations, has some valuable pointers for press cuttings.

Headings are based on three letters only: thus Accidents are ACC, Army is ARM, Agriculture is AGR. Subdivisions are of four letters, as CATT (Cattle), FERT (Fertilizers), etc. Thus we arrive at the code heading AGR: CATT for illustrations of Cattle. A similar system of country codes gives BEL (Belgium) BOR (Borneo) and so on.

Long winded headings used to describe files precisely are perhaps the only disadvantage that a name classification has over a numerical one for press cuttings.

Having considered the form of heading let us turn our attention to alphabetical order—not quite so simple as ABC after all! It is not difficult to sort a few words into alphabetical order. But when thousands of names and possibly several languages are involved the question becomes complex.

To begin with, there are two distinct kinds of alphabetical order—the 'all through' and the 'nothing before something' methods. When sorting by the 'all through' method the spaces between words are ignored and headings consisting of more than one word are treated as if they were run together. This gives the following:

SEA CADETS
SEALS
SEAMANSHIP
SEA SERPENTS
SEA SHELLS
SEAWEED

Applying the 'nothing before something' principle the blank space between the words is regarded as coming first in the alphabet, before the letter A, and the following order is obtained:

SEA CADETS
SEA SERPENTS
SEA SHELLS
SEALS
SEAMANSHIP
SEAWEED

In the second order, it is apparent, there is a tendency to bring together kindred subjects with the same prefatory heading—although too much weight should not be given to this. (It is not particularly helpful for example, to bring SEA CADETS and SEA SERPENTS together!)

In the main, the all through system is simpler to use but the nothing before something provides an element of classification. Nothing before something is useful with surnames since it brings names with similar prefixes together, but it falls down with personal names when it is not known if the name is spelt in two parts or not:

Le Grand	Defiant & Co.
Le Grove	De Haviland Ltd.
Leabank	Delany & Son
Legh	De La Rue
Lehane	

For further examples it is interesting to note that the Index to the *Encyclopaedia Britannica* is 'all through', as is *Kelly's Directory of Merchants Manufacturers and Shippers.*

In all, the order chosen is not of great significance. What *is* important is that everyone should understand *which* order is chosen, know how it works, and apply it consistently.

The punctuation and layout of headings on files is largely a matter of taste, the over-riding principle being clarity. The use of the colon to divide main and subheadings is neater than the ubiquitous dash. It may be used between main headings and subheadings but not between the words of an inverted heading nor to precede descriptive notes, where a comma is better, e.g.:

MEDALS: VICTORIA CROSS
but EUROPE, WEST
KENNEDY, JOHN P., *American President*

On all files forming subdivisions the main heading is repeated, of course, in order to fix its position in the sequence. Usually, the main heading appears on the left and the subheading on the right of the top edge of a folder. The complications of getting a series of descending subdivisions into a folder label are a further argument for limiting the number of steps of subdivision.

CHAPTER ELEVEN

Cross References

WE now come to the vitally important matter of cross references, without which the inquirer is like a traveller without maps or signposts. Broadly speaking, these are of two types, see references and see also references, the latter assuming a number of different forms.

The encyclopaedia method of arrangement used in smaller libraries, of simple headings in a single sequence, requires a great many see also references so as to bring together related material separated in the sequence. The larger library grouping under a smaller number of major divisions will require fewer references because part of the job of references has been taken over by the classification itself.

See references are used to guide the inquirer from where there is nothing filed to where it *is* filed: from all alternative headings to the heading chosen. Not only do they show where to look, they prevent similar material being filed under synonymous headings. So we may have NATURALIZATION see ALIENS, SWEEPSTAKES see LOTTERIES, FARMING see AGRICULTURE. See references are also used between alternative spellings, e.g. GYPSIES see GIPSIES, JUGOSLAVIA see YUGOSLAVIA; between other words of compound headings, e.g. DIVING, see SWIMMING AND DIVING; from antonyms, e.g. EMPLOYMENT see UNEMPLOYMENT; from the simple form to an inverted heading e.g. PUBLIC HEALTH see HEALTH, PUBLIC; from singular to plural forms, e.g. MOUSE see MICE; from alternative forms of personal name e.g. PHILIP, Prince see EDINBURGH, Duke of.

A strong case can be made out also for using see references as main headings leading to subdivisions, e.g. LIPSTICKS see

COSMETICS: LIPSTICKS; MANAGEMENT see INDUSTRY: MANAGEMENT. This is particularly necessary in libraries using the generic main class system. It is not usually thought worth while to employ references between subdivisions of the same main heading, however. It is unnecessary, for instance, to have LABOUR: DISPUTES see LABOUR: STRIKES.

See also references serve a different purpose. Whereas see references lead from an unused heading to a used one, see also references suggest where more material on related subjects may be found. By implication they also indicate, if negatively, the contents of a file, since they show what is not there. For example

ELECTORAL REFORM see also PROPORTIONAL REPRESENTATION

indicates that this aspect of electoral reform is filed away from the ELECTORAL REFORM heading. Or we might find under SUEZ CANAL, see also EGYPT: CANAL CRISIS 1956, indicating that the Suez crisis is filed with Egypt and not Suez Canal.

See also references act as a link between subjects and, as distinct from see references, sometimes appear in groups. For example:

REFUSE DISPOSAL
see also
DUSTMEN
LITTER
PAPER: SALVAGE
SCRAP METAL
SLAG HEAPS

LOCAL GOVERNMENT
see also
COUNTY COUNCILS
MAYORALTIES
PARISH COUNCILS
RATES

Further, they can form a chain. For example:

PACIFISM see also CONSCIENTIOUS OBJECTORS
CONSCIENTIOUS OBJECTORS see also PACIFISM

A really comprehensive network of see also references can tie up the loose ends of subject arrangement and assist the hurried inquirer with fresh ideas. In this connection the 'Here and Away' system of the *Radio Times* Hulton Picture Library could be more widely used. Each main heading is helpfully described as follows: (The headings are designed for illustrations, hence the different emphasis.)

JUVENILE (a main heading)

Here: Juvenile activities, baptisms, scouts, motherhood, creches, baby shows, children's costume.

Away: Toys in TOY, Juvenile labour in LAB, Customs in CUS, Childbirth and child welfare in MED, Juvenile crime in LAW, Day nurseries in EDU, Native and primitive children in TYP.

See also: Education, Home Life, Law, Medical, Misery and Poverty, Recreation, Religion, Sport, Toys, Women.

A final form of see also reference remains to be mentioned, the 'blanket' reference, used when referring from a general to a series of more specific headings, e.g.:

LABOUR

see also the subdivision LABOUR under specific countries and industries, as, FRANCE: LABOUR; TEXTILE INDUSTRY: LABOUR

We must also consider how these references should appear in the sequence. It is normal and useful to enter see also references on the files themselves. A limited number may appear on the outside front of the file, on the right hand upper face, so that they may quickly be seen. If at all extensive, however, provision has to be made for see also references on the inside of the file, possibly on the left-hand inside face of the file when it is opened. In the nature of things, see also references are always changing as headings change, and it is wise to enter references on a separate sheet, stapled to the file or in a pocket supplied for the purpose. On some files printed space is made available for references on the reverse.

See references appearing in the sequence should be entered on really strong cards and placed among the files. There are numerous objections, mainly on the ground that see reference cards become dirty, dog-eared and tend to slip down between the files. But nobody has yet invented a better method for on the spot reference.

As distinct from references between headings, a useful device is the slip reference (usually a see reference, taking the form of a note in the file, perhaps in its chronological place among the cuttings, indicating where a specific news story is filed. For example in SUBMARINE DIVING we might find a slip of paper saying 'for case of frogman Commander Crabbe and Russian Naval Vessels at PLYMOUTH see RUSSIA: NAVY.'

The system is useful, too, in biographical files, showing where incidents concerned with a man's life may be filed. For example:

> BENN, ANTHONY WEDGWOOD. For campaign to avoid peerage succession *see* PEERAGE: RELINQUISHMENT

The *Philadelphia Inquirer* uses a white printed slip 5 in × 3 in. in size, as follows:

PHILADELPHIA INQUIRER LIBRARY

For..

See..

A favoured form of slip reference is in the shape of a sample cutting from the story referred to with the reference appearing in the margin or on the mount. It is necessary clearly to mark the cutting REFERENCE ONLY so that the reference is not mistaken for the whole of the library's resources on the topic.

Considering the use of references as a whole it is not going too far to say that ample and imaginative references in the scheme of arrangement are more important than the choice of the scheme itself. Good references can make a poor scheme better and, in any library, make all the difference to rapid and successful service.

CHAPTER TWELVE

Schedules and Indexes

ALTHOUGH they are not universally used in news libraries, it is well worth while preparing a schedule of the subject headings in use, showing their arrangement and keeping it up to date. The schedule enables the scope of a section to be seen at a glance, anomalies and weaknesses are revealed, new topics can more easily be fitted into their proper places, and a true balance between subjects maintained. For a library which has not had one before the mere exercise of producing a schedule showing the order of subjects in the files is enormously beneficial and there are sure to be some surprises!

A schedule should be prepared on foolscap paper, not on index cards, so that the range of subdivisions can be seen together. The schedule may usefully include a number of cross references, as at *The Times*. Since it will be subject to constant amendment it is best typed on loose leaf sheets, allowing a page or so at a time to be retyped when the quantity of handwritten notes or alterations tends to get out of hand. For they certainly will!

A further key to the collection—also seldom fully used but worth all the time spent on it, is an index to the subject files. Whereas the schedule is a map, displaying the scheme as it exists on the ground, the index is a gazeteer, listing all headings and subheadings, all subjects covered, with full see and see also references, in one alphabetical sequence. This is the order of the encyclopaedia, as used in smaller collections as we have remarked earlier. With such an arrangement of files an index becomes less necessary, although a schedule of headings remains important.

The larger libraries with more complete schemes and changing staffs would find such a subject index invaluable. For the generic class arrangement it is essential. Once compiled it is difficult to understand how the library survived without it. It serves a number of purposes, not the least of which is to act as a check against lost files. Without an index or a schedule it would not be impossible for a little used file to disappear altogether and for no one to realize that the library had ever had it. Principally, however, it is a means of speeding up research. It is quicker to examine an index to discover the whereabouts of a topic than to search several places in the sequence for it.

The subject index is best arranged on cards—5 in. × 3 in. is large enough—allowing an infinite number of new cards and changes to be made without difficulty. Every file is represented by a card. The index should be fully cross referenced, preferably with see reference cards of a different colour to distinguish them from file-headings.

Thus a sequence might read:

SOUTH EAST ASIA: DEFENCE
SOUTH EAST ASIA ECONOMIC CONDITIONS
SOUTH EAST ASIA: MINORITIES
SOUTHPORT, Lancs, see MUNICIPALITIES: SOUTHPORT
SOVIET RUSSIA see RUSSIA
SPACE TRAVEL see INTERPLANETARY TRAVEL
MOON
ROCKETS AND MISSILES
SPAIN: CHURCH
SPAIN: FINANCE
SPAIN: FOREIGN RELATIONS
etc.

There is no reason why, if time permits, cards representing biographical files should not also be used in the same sequence, although it is more usual to keep these separately. The amount of work involved in making out cards for every new file is not heavy once the basic sequence has been made.

Where an index of subjects and references is in use it does, of course, largely overcome the need for references in the files. A number of these are still useful but the problem of the continual alteration of references on permanent files is largely overcome by using cards in their place. *The Guardian* library employs cards of a distinctive colour in its subject index to headings so as to refer to specific news stories, rather as slip references were described in the previous chapter.

Cards have one further considerable advantage over references on files. It is possible to show on the reverse side of cards representing files what references are made *to* them—known as tracings. Thus the main card AGRICULTURE may bear on the reverse:

See refs from FARMING
See also refs from COUNTRYSIDE PRESERVATION
CROWN LANDS
FOOD SUPPLIES
HOUSING: TIED COTTAGES
LAND

With changing headings some such system is absolutely essential. Otherwise when a file heading is drastically altered to keep up with changed usage it is likely that the old references to it will be overlooked and inquirers will be referred to gaps in the sequence.

Index cards should carry the same heading precisely as the file they represent. They can also be used to carry brief notes about their subject which aim at satisfying simple inquiries without reference to the file itself. For example, cards may answer commonly asked questions such as

SUMMER TIME

Clocks forward	22 March, 1964
Clocks back	25 October, 1964

Biographical cards may bear dates of birth and death, or lists of appointments with dates. Topographical notes may be added to place names. The precise contents of a subject file may be noted: as we have seen, it is sometimes as useful to say what is *not* in a file as what *is* in it. For example,

> DRUGS
>
> Includes drug addiction only
> Medicinal drugs in
> MEDICINES A–Z.

All these things are time consuming, but if there *is* the time available they soon prove their worth. A schedule *and* an index is ideal. A schedule alone is good. An index alone is better. In any event, some form of key or control of its contents is essential for good library management.

CHAPTER THIRTEEN

Discarding

SUCCESSFUL discarding is certainly the dullest and also one of the most difficult tasks in a library of press cuttings. Yet it must be done: frequently, with regularity, and according to some principles. It also needs a little courage, for from time to time some of the material thrown away is sure to be asked for.

To retain cuttings 'because they may come in useful sometime' does no service to anyone and merely adds bulk of doubtful value to the files. The proper answer to those asking for something that has just been thrown away is that it is now in demand for the first time in several years and such rare use does not justify its occupation of precious space.

The news library should regard itself as a pool in a flowing river of news. Everything flows in, to be held for a time, eventually to pass on, either into books and indexes, or into limbo. The question is: how long should cuttings be retained and what classes of material can most safely be discarded first? Thus put in general terms the question is almost unanswerable, for the reply will be different for each library and can only be decided by experience.

The Press Library of the Royal Institute of International Affairs, for example, has been in existence since 1924 and has never thrown anything away. But then, its purpose is different from that of news libraries used primarily by students taking a long term view. The *Daily Telegraph* cuttings date from about 1928 and none of the home newspaper material has been discarded. At the Press Association, on the other hand, regular discarding is going on all the time, so that roughly as much is thrown away in a year as is put in. It is plain that for most news libraries regular discarding is essential and we should be able to offer some suggestions.

We must suppose that the library is not regarded as a repository for historical records. If this is so, clearly, different rules will apply and a good deal more space will be needed. Perhaps an arrangement can be made with a library concerned with the long term preservation of material for acceptance of cuttings from the library. Experience teaches, however, that while many may deplore the discarding process, few are prepared to offer house room to mitigate its effects.

Any news librarian will agree that by far the heaviest demand for information and cuttings relates to events of the last six months, the six months before that it is sharply reduced, to be further reduced after another year, and so on at an increasing rate until cuttings five years old and more are rarely used indeed. But they are wanted sometimes. It is the difficult task of the librarian to decide at what point usage tails off to such a degree that cuttings are no longer worth the space they occupy.

Some events, of course, age more quickly than others. For this reason, it is not practicable strictly to apply a rule limiting all material to (say) five years only. It is, however, useful to have such a term as a guide—and to let it be known among library users that (generally speaking) the library covers such period and no more.

Plans for discarding may begin as soon as items are added to the collection. To a limited degree it is possible to file certain types of cuttings under a temporary heading, sometimes labelled 'Pickle'. This in effect forms a Temporary Section and it is confined to certain distinct purposes. Thus, announcements of forthcoming events can form part of it until the event is over, proceedings in lower courts can be filed here until the Higher Court hearing, minor street accidents, and anything else for which there is an occasional immediate demand unlikely to be repeated. It is convenient to have a section where discarding can be drastic provided the rules for what goes in it are clear.

Less successful are attempts to stamp a T for Temporary on a loosely defined range of cuttings at the outset and to file them with others in the normal sequence. The 'T' is supposed to make discarding easier when the time comes. In fact, of course, it is well nigh impossible to forecast what general cuttings will and will not be required later and the 'T' may prove a snare.

The actual business of discarding takes two forms: the thinning of files by discarding valueless cuttings from them, and the discarding of the files themselves. A steady and continuous routine thinning of files can, over a period, save a good deal of space and enable basic material to be retained longer. The job is undoubtedly a bore and has to be done with mature judgement. A little and often is the best approach—perhaps not more than an hour a day provided it is every day. Too long leads to tedium and thoughtless decisions. Here and there one finds libraries fortunate enough to be able to employ ex-members of the staff part-time to weed specific sections, but it must be emphasized that the job requires experience.

The kind of subjects which lend themselves to thinning are those now closed but not yet unwanted: the biographical files of the recently dead, many of the lightweight cuttings of a topic heavily written about but now completed (a major earthquake, Suez, Election campaigning). A few meaty feature articles with a round-up of facts are a useful insurance against excess of zeal.

More immediately effective is the discarding of files themselves. It can sometimes be decided that a whole topic no longer justifies the space it occupies. Often, it must be confessed, the decision is made more urgent by pressure on space in a certain section, but pressure of this kind can lead to dangerous decisions and discarding for the wrong reasons.

This is made easier if the scheme of arrangement allows a measure of chronological subdivision. Some big subjects, i.e. Unemployment, United Nations plenary sessions, can be arranged in this way and thus the earlier files in the sequence conveniently lend themselves to discarding.

After a time it becomes necessary to take really big decisions, like abandoning all files on the Korean War, or certain U.S. Presidential Election material. Factors bearing on the decision include the availability of the material in other forms or elsewhere. The library may index newspapers as well as cut them and, where this is the case, it obviously feels a good deal freer over discarding. The ready accessibility of *The Times Index* and bound or microfilmed copies of *The Times* have a similar effect. To a lesser degree, the gathering of the subject in book form is a factor.

It must be remembered, however, that much of the material about to be thrown away is unique and irreplaceable. Not all of it will be indexed and books provide only a widely meshed net. Moreover, many news libraries are expected to give rapid service, often late at night when other sources of information are closed. The library thus has to be as self-contained as possible and this is bound to inhibit over-bold discarding.

It is here that the library with a little space to spare in which to store discarded files is blessed. A basement, an attic, a room across the street, can save the day. With this safeguard, discarded files can be stored away from the main sequence for perhaps another few years before final abandonment, and retrieved if necessary from the consequences of a too-rash decision. Among these happy folk is the librarian of the *Financial Times* who has the use of an extensive basement into which go all discarded files and out-of-date reference books. Similarly, the *New York Times* library maintains files covering a thirty-year period (longer than most) in active use and earlier matter is stored in another floor. The *Daily Mirror*, also, makes use of storage space for less used material on the floor above the main library.

At the *Financial Times* subject cuttings are retained for seven years. A new file is made for every subject every year. Two or three superseded files are retained next to the current file. Earlier than that, material goes into the basement. The Reuter Library, which dates in its present form from 1944, maintains a separate sequence of less-frequently used cuttings and Reuter messages in pamphlet boxes after the material has been removed from the main sequence of lateral files. From this sequence, drastic discarding can be made as necessary. At the *Daily Telegraph*, where space is equally pressing, the problem is dealt with by gradually removing from earlier files all non-*Telegraph* items, and by reducing the intake from newspapers other than the *Daily Telegraph* and *Sunday Telegraph*.

Approaching the question from a slightly different point of view, Mr E. J. C. Smythe, then Librarian of *Reynolds News* (now *Sunday Citizen*), writing in Aslib Proceedings in 1949, referred to special treatment given to cuttings intended for permanent filing. After a year they are bound in spring back binders in order of subjects, indexed and titled, and placed on shelves like books. The library employs an interesting chronological method of arrangement for less permanent material which assists discarding.

To each file one year's cuttings are allowed and no more. At the end of a year the cuttings are taken from the open folder and placed in envelopes. The envelope is then marked with the subject and the year and filed either directly behind the open folder in the stacks if there is room or elsewhere.

It is perhaps necessary to emphasize that the decision over what shall be discarded must be the librarian's alone. Only he is in a position to balance all the factors bearing on the decision, usually an assessment of the potential value of the item against the value of the space it occupies. To bring in a member of the editorial staff or someone else not connected with the library is wrong on all counts. He may know the topic under review but he is not familiar with library requirements. He cannot know what duplicate or alternative records are available. He is certain to judge subjectively in the light of his own needs, and he is not in the position of the librarian who is better able to forecast the degree of demand from several quarters. Since the librarian has the ultimate responsibility he must have the authority also. In any event, he is sure to be blamed in the end.

CHAPTER FOURTEEN

Newspaper Indexing

WE have considered at some length the problems of press cuttings as sources of information. It may reasonably be asked whether it would not be better to abandon these untidy slips of paper altogether and index the newspaper instead. For some purposes it may be so. Many libraries employ a combination of indexing and cutting newspapers to provide current information, although generally the emphasis is on cuttings.

A characteristic of an index is that, once made, it is permanent and not subject to change. It takes up less space than cuttings and nothing need be discarded from it on these grounds. Indeed, such is the labour of making it and the importance and uniqueness of its coverage, that it will be kept for ever, still useful in some ways even if it is divorced from the printed material it refers to.

Normally, the indexed newspapers must themselves be retained, of course, but in many organizations this would be the case whether they were indexed or not. Where these are available on microfilm the space problem is largely overcome. Very often, when the inquiry is merely for a date or a name, a good index can supply the information without reference to the files. On the other hand, it must be admitted that this is the exception and, in general, two processes are necessary to use the index. First consult the index, then turn up the reference. It may be the wrong one, making it necessary to look again.

The physical form of an index imposes a limit on the period it can cover in one sequence and cumulations over more than a year are seldom practicable. Accordingly, a single index cannot show the development of a subject like a file of cuttings—each reference has to be separately examined and sometimes reference to several annual or monthly cumulations may be necessary.

Bound files are heavy and microfilm can be clumsy, all of which adds up to making an index less convenient in use than cuttings. For the specific item of which the approximate date is known it works well. For a broad view or 'background' it is less satisfactory.

As we have noted, the index need not be comprehensive of the whole newspaper, but can if required be employed to cover specific aspects of news or styles of presentation. One of the most useful of these is an index of names. The *Financial Times* has an annual name index on 5 in. × 3 in. cards including an ingenious system of coloured tab markers indicating death, so that these may be removed from the 'live' sequence at the end of the year before the remainder of the cards are accumulated with previous sequences.

Elsewhere, indexes of sports results, letters to the editor by author, company meetings, or certain types of feature or leading articles are useful.

The Guardian both indexes and cuts its own newspaper in considerable detail. Among the most convenient of the unpublished newspaper indexes are those of the *Daily Mail*, *Daily Sketch*, and *Evening News*, all prepared to the same plan. These take the form of a comprehensive index to all editions on typed sheets bound annually in volumes. The volume A–C of the *Daily Mail* is foolscap in size and 5 or 6 in. thick.

Another excellent subject index is that of the *Financial Times*, which takes the form in the current year of 10 in. × 4½ in. slips filed overlapping each other with visible lower margins in heavy guarded loose leaf ledgers of the type commonly used for sales records. Entries are inscribed on these in accordance with a prepared series of detailed subject headings. At the end of the year the slips are transferred to sheaf binders where several years' entries are cumulated in one sequence.

It is necessary to make newspaper indexing an entirely separate task from the other routine processes of library, with a staff working on this exclusively. This occurs because the physical approach to the job is quite distinct from that of cuttings. A separate set of newspapers is necessary. To try and link indexing with cutting by indexing from prepared cuttings is not usually successful.

Apart from *The Times Index*, and the little known index to the *Glasgow Herald*, no British newspaper index is published, so we will regard indexes in this chapter as unpublished, prepared by typewriter or in manuscript, for the internal use of the library. This enables a number of short cuts and savings to be made.

As to physical shape, there can be few libraries still indexing in those heavy leather-bound volumes which were the valued repositories of newspaper index references of time gone by. Their failure, of course, was rigidity, so that once a sequence had taken up its allotted space you were stuck, and it was impossible to fit unexpected new alphabetical headings in their proper places. The successors of these ledgers are annual cumulations of sheets typed in foolscap from index slips or cards like those we have referred to at the *Daily Mail* and its sister papers. Only when entries have ceased is it possible to bind.

It is on these slips or cards that most schemes of indexing depend.

With the use of slips—quite small pieces of thin paper, perhaps 5 in. × 2 in. in size—one entry is made on each slip, allotted a heading and filed in its alphabetical place after the indexing is completed. More than one entry can be made on each slip if preferred, but the time factor of finding the slip and removing it from the sequence, and replacing it later, has to be taken into account.

The slips take up minimum space in shallow drawers (described in Chapter Two). Provided the script is legible, they can be prepared by hand, which is generally quicker than inserting and removing them from a typewriter. The waste of time involved in removing slips from a typewriter is reduced by the use of ribbons of slips joined by perforations. When torn apart after indexing, however, the perforation is a nuisance and renders consultation difficult. The slips are consulted in their primary form for the current period—usually a year. After the end of that time they are transcribed on to sheets and bound in volumes. Basically, this is the method of the printed index before the type-setting stage.

The flimsiness of the slips is no disadvantage since they are not expected to last long. By the year's end there is a very large quantity of them, but since they are soon to be discarded and replaced in the drawers by a new sequence the space is unimportant. The transcribing process on to sheets, however, is lengthy and requires minute checking. Even so, the possibility of error is doubled. Experiments now being made to reproduce the entries by photographic methods appear to offer some promise.

An alternative is an index prepared on stiff cards, which are expected to last. This is the method of *The Guardian* index, which goes back, in various forms, to the middle of the last century.

These cards, like the slips, are hived off at the end of a year but remain in their trays as when the last entry was made on them. A new set of trays and new cards starts the new year. Because thicker cards take up more space and they remain in the library indefinitely, cards usually hold a number of references until full, extensive subjects taking up several cards, all fully used. The long-term use needs typed references for clarity and the cards have to be withdrawn from the sequence and replaced after every new entry. All of which takes a good deal longer than the slip system—but no transcription is necessary at the year's end. The B.B.C. news bulletins are fully indexed in this way.

Whichever of the foregoing methods is chosen has a bearing on the classification of entries. It is generally said that the cardinal principle of good indexing is specific entry. This can be done with slips, each new entry being filed under the narrowest heading that will contain it and a new heading made out even if it embraces only a single item. Thus an index compiled on slips is likely to be narrower in its headings than the classification scheme for cuttings. In its purest form specific entry gets right away from the headings for cuttings and the two are by no means interchangeable. It is important, nevertheless, that the headings chosen and the method of arrangement be in as close accord with the cuttings collection as practicable. Good indexing under specific headings requires a degree of skill and, of course, absolute accuracy.

As we have seen, entries on permanent cards have a space factor to consider. An infinite number of cards, each with one reference, is far too prodigal of space and would be equivalent to giving each cutting a separate file in the cuttings sequence. So in the case of cards, the material is entered to a sequence of prepared headings, rather as cuttings are filed. No hesitation should be made over new headings where appropriate but the result, unavoidably, is a broader division. It may well be, also, that this arrangement suits certain kinds of inquiry best—showing the scope of a subject more successfully than specific entry is able to do.

Under the slip entry system we would have this (taken from *The Times Index*):

ELECTRICAL INDUSTRY
  Labour
    Disputes
      E.T.U. statement
      Guerilla tactics
      Pickets at power stations
} Three slips used to index

Under the card system, in contrast, we might employ one card only, to be retained permanently like the following example from *The Guardian* Index.

```
BRITISH GUIANA  (3)

 State of emergency declared          May 23 p1 c1
 Sentry go on the sugar estates (LEADER)
                                      May 25 p8 c1
 Two racial murders.  British army units arrive
                                      May 25 p9 c6
 East Indian refugees shipped from Mackenzie
                                      May 27 p11 c6
```

```
INDUSTRY : MANAGEMENT : EDUCATION & TRAINING (7)
 Business school at Liverpool Univ. (Own Rep)
                                      Oct 19 p4 c6
 BIM survey - "The Making of Managers"
                                      Nov 19 p13 c3
 Franks Report - "British Business Schools"
                   (Industrial staff) Nov 27 p4 c3
 Schools of business management (LEADER)
                                      Nov 27 p10 c1
 FBI supports recommendations in Franks Report
                                      Dec 12 p16 c4
```

Courtesy of The Guardian

In order to miss nothing in the newspaper under examination, the indexer should start on page one at the top of the left-hand column and work through the page from left to right, up and down, a column at a time. The process continues—page by page—covering all of the paper required for indexing.

The essential information to be given in all index entries is the same, although the more specific the heading the less the need for description of the item indexed. In its fullest form the news item is scanned by the indexer and its parts isolated. It will need a main entry, with possible additional entries under branch topics dealt with lower down the column. If required, personal names will be indexed also. It is helpful to underline key words indicating headings on first reading of the item.

Each slip must bear the appropriate subheading along the top edge in case it becomes misplaced.

Entries should be as brief and as informative as possible with no words wasted. Perhaps the subject heading alone is sufficient, for example:

EARTHQUAKES: Tunisia

Or the point of the topic may briefly be paraphrased, e.g.:

ELECTRICITY INDUSTRY	PRESS
Labour	Freedom of
Wages offer	J. Freeman: Speech
Unions fail to agree	to Institute of Journalists

The use of quoted headlines to identify the item is tempting. This is easier for unskilled indexers and for two thirds of the time it works. But headlines can be misleading and they usually concentrate only on one aspect of the story. Further, they may change between editions.

Finally, each entry must bear date, page, and column reference, plus the edition if other than the last. Various abbreviations may be used—all designed to save space, e.g.:

Apl3^{xx} p 3 c 2
or 3/IV^{xx} 3:2 } April 3rd. Two star edition, page 3 column 2.

Newspaper stories sometimes move about the page and from one page to another in different editions. A number of news items appear in certain editions only. It is usual to index the final edition first, giving page and column reference relating to this edition. All entries bearing no distinguishing mark are regarded as from the final edition. The indexer then works from the final back towards the first edition giving the latest placing for those items in earlier editions only—with, of course, a symbol indicating which edition they appeared in.

References should be fairly lavishly provided, on the same basis as described in Chapter Eleven for cuttings. Single items require duplicate or multiple entry, not references. Continuing topics require references rather than multiple entry so as to save space.

A difficult problem of referencing in indexes is that of changed names and varying news emphasis leading to different headings and, consequently, changed references. When a heading alters, a see reference is placed at the old heading and a retrospective reference at the new, e.g.

> SEVERN CATCHMENT BOARD
> For continuation of this subject see
> SEVERN RIVER BOARD

and

> SEVERN RIVER BOARD
> For earlier references see SEVERN CATCHMENT BOARD

This works in the year in question. For the inquirer examining indexes of earlier years and moving forward, however, the heading may disappear from his sight unless he comes across the relevant period in which the change took place. It is too late to place references in earlier bound sequences: in future sequences it is forgotten or regarded as unnecessary. Accordingly, change of headings—especially in printed indexes—can cause more problems than it solves and is usually undertaken at the last possible moment.

The chief published newspaper index in this country is that of *The Times*, which is issued in two-monthly volumes but not cumulated. *The Times Index* dates from 1906. Before this period

Palmer's *Index to the Times* is available covering the period 1868 to 1943 and carried back to 1790.

The relatively short period covered by each volume nowadays enables the index to be issued rather than if it were published say quarterly (as it was until 1956) or annually. Nevertheless, the issue of six separate volumes each year makes consultation over a long period a laborious affair.

The indexing itself, however, is excellent. It does not always accord with the canons of formal indexing, but it does the job fully and economically. It is a major bibliographical achievement which goes unaccountably without full credit.

The *Index* is prepared by a small staff who work on this task exclusively. It is regarded as a separate operation within *The Times* Intelligence Dept. Entries are written by hand on $5\frac{3}{8}$ in. × $6\frac{7}{8}$ in. slips of white bank paper, a separate slip for each item. A certain degree of specialization is possible among the indexers into sport, financial and obituary pages, and so on. The slips are later filed with appropriate references in the bundles for the same subject on previous days in pamphlet boxes which contain copy which, in due course, will go to the printer. Before printing, slips are edited to excise superfluous words.

The *Times Index* exemplifies one of the problems of comprehensive name indexing. Although, normally, all personal names are indexed, it is neither possible nor desirable to enter all mentions of (say) the Prime Minister under his name. Some discretion has to be allowed to the indexer.

The *Glasgow Herald* is the only other British newspaper to publish an index. It is issued annually and dates from 1906. Entries are grouped broadly with only limited subdivision, on the basis of the card entry system described earlier in this chapter.

Equal in achievement to *The Times Index* is the *Index to the New York Times*, a work of elaborate coverage published every two weeks and cumulated annually. It is claimed for the *New York Times* annual indexes that they are the only reference source in existence that classifies and summarises world news of the past century alphabetically by subject, persons, organizations, and geographical locations. The earlier volumes of the index are long out of print but it is planned to reprint the series, 1851–1961. At the time of writing the 1930–40 indexes are available and 1941 to 1961 will shortly be ready. The volumes 1913–29 will follow in sequence.

CHAPTER FIFTEEN

Supplementary Records

THIS is a chapter of odds and ends—but useful ones. It will be evident by now that a news library is a repository not only of the great events of our times but of the little things, small, human, sometimes unusual, which make life so interesting.

In the main, the news library preserves these facts on record in the form of cuttings in several great sections or sequences of the library. Aside from these, however, a number of special lists and indexes can be maintained which, as well as helping to answer inquiries from unusual points of view, go to make the library a positive news service, assisting from time to time in the making of news as well as recording it. Most of these records will be prepared on cards, although some can take the form of special information files of actual materials.

Let us examine some of the possibilities.

Standard Information Index

Rapid service is important and certain inquiries tend to repeat themselves. So it is helpful to build up an index of standard information and commonly asked questions. The index is arranged by subjects and includes such facts as the dates of opening and admission to notable places, times of certain ceremonies, areas and heights of well-known buildings and geographical features, local populations and statistics, dates of summer time, area of sports pitches, little known and new groups of initials, and a mass of other heterogeneous information constantly in demand. The value of the index is well worth the trouble of keeping up to date. The criterion of selection should not be too rigid: catholicity, imagination and forethought are required in its compilation. It need hardly be said, however, that there is no need to repeat in it such facts as are readily available from *Whitaker's Almanack* or some other obvious source.

Index of Societies

Names and addresses of secretaries and officials of societies are always in demand and often hard to come by. The smaller societies have no office address or telephone number and officials are always changing. Changes and names can usefully be watched for in the day's news and recorded on cards arranged either alphabetically by title of the organization or by subject interest. An immensely useful source for society officials are printed letter headings. Such letters reach newspaper and similar bodies in large numbers, and the library may usefully make arrangements to record the information on the letter heading after use in the appropriate department. The date of the information is important and this should be shown on the card.

Index of Experts

Societies' officials are important as sources of information. In the same category are 'experts'. No library is omniscient, even if it makes a brave try at it, and some kinds of information (technical, medical) are better sought direct from the expert than from printed sources. The goodwill and mutual assistance of specialists and organizations should be assiduously cultivated and often the library can reciprocate the help it seeks suddenly by telephone. An experts or 'contacts' index arranged by subject can be filed in the same sequence as the societies.

Index to Sources

In spite of imposing bibliographies each librarian nevertheless has to carry in his head a list of reference books and their contents, and try to remember unexpected places where information can be found. An index to sources, combined perhaps with a location index to current information, is worth building up. It is merely a matter of noting a useful reference—some unexpected item to be found in a set of statistical tables, perhaps—wherever it appears, and listing it under subjects. The staff may be encouraged to note here the sources of inquiries answered after some difficulty. For example:

ROYAL COMMISSIONS
A list of Royal Commissions 1900–62 appears in:
WHERE TO LOOK FOR YOUR LAW

NEWSPAPERS
Per head of population *see* Unesco Communications handbook

FOREIGN AMBASSADORS IN LONDON
see Diplomatic List
International Year Book

Chairman's List

It is the fashion that governmental reports such as tribunals and royal commissions come to be known by the names of their chairmen. Government documentation is not awfully good at titles of reports and the name of the chairman of a board of inquiry not only provides a convenient shorthand means of referring to it but allows on occasion a nice display of conversational one-up-manship. Most of us can probably identify the

Pilkington Report, the Roberts Report, or the Radcliffe Report. But what subjects did the Parry or Priestley Reports cover?*

A list of such chairmen, giving the short title and location of their reports, may save the library from the embarrassment of admitting ignorance. No matter how well-known the report appears to be at the time, index it. It soon slips out of mind.

Chairmen are listed, of course, in the indexes to H.M.S.O. lists of government publications. But searching monthly issues is laborious and few news libraries seem to stock them.

Coming Events

This is commonly not an index but a sequence of files arranged by subject or chronologically. Alternatively, it may be a large wall calendar. It is a supplement (possibly a better one) to those items collected by harrassed news editors who cut these for themselves, placing them in a diary as a reminder of stories to cover each day. A lively news library is not expected always to be absorbed in the past but should on occasion be able to give such particulars as are published of any approaching event. Every library is likely to be asked, and should be able to answer from time to time such questions as the date of the Motor Show or the visit of some international celebrity. This is one of the few occasions when advertisements are worth cutting. (If the event is likely to be prominent it will, of course, rank for a heading in the main sequence, with a reference in Coming Events.)

* For those who have forgotten:

Parry	British Guiana
Priestley	Civil Service
Roberts	Library Services
Pilkington	Doctors' and Dentists' Remuneration *or* Television

Radcliffe means different things to different sections of the community. Recently it meant the Vassall inquiry but there were several earlier reports, on taxation and on county courts by different men of the same name.

Anniversaries Register

Another kind of coming event, which the interested librarian can ferret out for himself, is the approaching anniversary, centenary or similar occasion for comment. News libraries serving publishing organizations have a steady call for this class of information from feature writers and the library can make a positive contribution by drawing attention to such events. (*The Times* publishes a good list at the beginning of each year.)

Local Diary

The provincial news library is in itself a major source of reference on recent local events. If there is time it can be rewarding to keep a diary, brief factual notes on local events as they occur. This is sometimes useful in preparing 'annual reviews' at the end of the year and as time goes by each year's diary becomes increasingly valuable.

'Local Associations'

Not societies again, but a phrase which can be usefully added to biographical files or to the biographical index of small provincial libraries. Some compile indexes to local authors, theatre folk, and artists arranged by occupation for the sake of the 'local angle', a matter of prime importance to regional libraries.

Subject Index to Biography

The usefulness of this has already been touched on (Chapter Seven). It does not attempt to cover all subjects—there is no value in a list of all British politicians in the library, for example. But some find it useful to have such a key to certain narrow categories separated in the normal alphabetical sequence. Thus the subject index may maintain current lists of all Hapsburgs, Roman Catholic cardinals, mountaineers, explorers, or other special groups which may be wanted together.

Pioneers

One of the most interesting supplementary files is a list on cards of 'pioneers'—any person who can claim to be the first to do anything at all, together with brief details and, of course, the date. The record includes recent as well as long past achievements and can be added to with surprising frequency. One of these at the *Guardian—Journal* in Nottingham included at one time the first man to wear a straw hat , the first man to carry an umbrella, the first English girl to marry a G.I. in the last war, the first tiled roof, the first bomb to fall on Nottinghamshire, and so on. Useless information? Perhaps. But the reader who has followed these pages thus far will be aware that such odd facts have value in the press and broadcasting services when used in the right way. In some libraries the 'Pioneer File' is extended to 'First and Last', adding to the record a number of final occasions.

The list is by no means exhausted and any news library may add a few more for its particular needs, or combine several of the foregoing into one. A list of prospective parliamentary candidates is useful, for instance. Or a key to the family names of newly-elected peers who have taken place names as titles. (Who on earth, we were saying at one time, is Lord Netherthorpe?*) A key to the terms of treaties is another.

The Reuter Library makes good use of supplementary records. In addition to some of the suggestions already made in this chapter the library maintains a series of folders entitled 'Special lists and Chronologies'. These take the form of typed schedules, with dates, including:

Air Crashes (over 50 dead)
Assassinations
Atomic Explosions
Earthquakes (over 1,000 dead)
Lord Mayors of London

* Formerly Sir James Turner, of the National Farmers Union.

Royal Visits
Space Flights (manned)
Space Flights (unmanned)
Vetoes in the Security Council
etc.

The library also employs a strip index of events and dates entitled 'When was that?' Similar lists are in use at the Press Association.

There is the further need already mentioned to maintain special files for a time in support of a particular policy or a forthcoming feature article. Some of these are better arranged as index references: pressure groups, for example, road accidents on motorways, mail bag robberies on railways, and so forth. Many such collections can be dispensed with when their immediate purpose has been served.

CHAPTER SIXTEEN

Books, Pamphlets, and Bound Files

(i) BOOKS

WHILE the main source material of a news library is press cuttings, it is necessary to provide a sufficient number of reference books in addition, reinforcing the collection and providing basic information and background. Many newspaper reports are hurriedly prepared and although undeniably containing the most recent information on a subject their accuracy should never be regarded as absolute. Wherever possible, cuttings should be referred to in conjunction with books. The best way to encourage this is to have a first rate collection of reference books close at hand.

It need not be extensive. It should consist mainly of quick reference books—similar to the quick reference section of a good public library—supplemented by a strong local collection where applicable and a number of standard works. We have to remember that although the news library book collection cannot hope to compete with the public reference library in this field, it must maintain a representative selection, in order to ensure the relative self-sufficiency we have already referred to.

This means that, as a minimum, the news library must have access to a couple of good encyclopaedias, a number of international reference books on current affairs, and up-to-date trade directories and year books for as many industries and professions as possible. Professional lists are in demand (RIBA *Kalendar*, *Crockford*, and so on) and there is no limit to the number of biographical reference books required. The monthly *Current Biography* is practically indispensible, as are all the *Who's Whos*. Quotations are important and it is necessary to stock a number of such collections (both of the kind with an index of key words for tracing sources and those classified by subjects and much used by worried journalists in search of an apt quotation to embellish an arid story). The handbooks of the sporting associations provide an important source for those concerned with the subject. Ideally, the aim should be a reference work on every likely topic—particularly in the humanities, but with the low value placed on books in most current information collections this is perhaps asking too much. The provincial news library has an obvious need for local trade and street directories and as much local history as possible. As a further source of names, electoral lists are useful, plus a set of British telephone directories.

Few news libraries achieve these modest aims in full. It is remarkable, however, what can be done with a thorough acquaintance with *Who's Who*, *Whitaker*, and a good encyclopaedia.

There is little point in offering a full list of the reference books which are useful. A good basic collection can be drawn up by visiting a public reference library with a good quick reference section on the open shelves and with the aid of a good modern bibliography. Walford's *Guide to Reference Material*. 1959, and *Supplement*, 1963, are probably best for this purpose. Experience of day-to-day needs soon indicates further requirements.

In these days of rapid change few printed works are still up to date when published. In the case of annuals, which stay on the shelves only a year, there is much to be said for a modest programme of amendments by pasting cuttings in the margins and altering names and appointments neatly in ink. Such amendments should not be too lavish or the books will soon become over-stuffed with cuttings, breaking the bindings and rendering them unpleasant to handle. Some books which may usefully be amended in this way include:

Whitaker's Almanack	Cabinet changes
	Ministerial changes
	New sporting records

Statesman's Year Book	Foreign governments and officials Treaty terms
Who's Who *International Who's Who*	Record all deaths with dates
The Times House of Commons *Vacher's or Dod's Parliamentary Companion*	Changes in representation By-election results Candidates (not forgetting to amend the index of *The Times H of C*)
Municipal Year Book	New mayors, town clerks
Crockford's Clerical Directory (or local Diocesan directories)	Changes in incumbents, or rank of clergy
Foreign Office List and *CRO List*	New ambassadors, High Commissioners and Governors

The *Financial Times* amends the *Directory of Directors* daily. Instead of merely amending the *Statesman's Year Book*, the Reuter Library maintains, on horizontal card trays employing the visible edge principle, a list of foreign governments which is kept up to date. Thus the answer to our earlier question 'who has taken over in Zanzibar?' is readily available.

Whatever the size of the book collection some form of catalogue or list of volumes is necessary. It is best prepared on 5 in. × 3 in. cards. For the larger collection a catalogue serves three purposes. It lists books under subjects and thus provides an added source for inquiries, it serves as a location directory for the books, and it serves as a check list against volumes going astray. For the small collection of a dozen or so shelves, its purpose is chiefly the latter. Without a catalogue a book can go missing and no one realize the library ever had it.

Librarians whose chief concern is books have codified the principles of cataloguing. For the news library a very simple form is adequate, but it is as well to abide by a set of rules to ensure consistency. Two entries per book are usually sufficient for directories, under subject and under title. (Directories, annuals, and many other quick reference books do not lend themselves to entry under authors.) It is enough to record the title, date of publication, and a location mark under the title entry, the subject entry being identical except for the addition of the subject to the top of the card, e.g.

NEWSPAPER PRESS DIRECTORY	070
1964	

PRESS	070
Newspaper Press Directory	
1964	

Annuals on standing order do not need a card every year. The date of the current volume should be entered in pencil with the earlier date erased if the superseded volume is to be discarded.

The news library may find itself responsible also for numerous copies of desk books like *Who's Who*, heavily used and located outside the library. Under these circumstances a catalogue is even more essential, showing the number of copies in use and their location.

Catalogue cards are occasionally arranged in the same sequence of cards as the subject index to the cuttings, thus reducing the number of separate card indexes in use and drawing maximum attention to more than one kind of material on the same subject. Where this is done cards representing other material than press cuttings may be distinguished by colour.

Those libraries with larger book collections running to some thousands of volumes will find it useful to arrange by one of the classification schemes devised for books, such as the Dewey Decimal System. The system requires careful study and a good deal of experience before it can be properly used, however. On the other hand, attempts to classify books in the same order as the alphabetical scheme of the cuttings do not work, owing to the different approach of the two kinds of material. For directories a perfectly satisfactory but arbitrary system consists of numerical symbols of three or four figures, grouping material by subject. Thus

2 Trade directories
25 Electrical trade
252 B.E.A.M.A. Catalogue

A key to the system should be prominently displayed near the books. A visible strip index works well and can easily be amended.

It goes without saying that all books should be clearly stamped as the property of the library. The best position is along the top edge of the book.

(ii) PAMPHLETS

Quantities of pamphlets descend free of charge and unasked on news organizations, and the librarian should see to it that all of these eventually reach the library and that the more useful of them are retained in the collection. They are important for the same reason as cuttings: they give the latest information or view on a subject, usually in easy to read form.

What is a pamphlet? It is defined as a document of less than 50 pages, stitched, but not bound, with a paper or thin card cover. There are other variants. None of them are particularly helpful. The important characteristic is that it is too flimsy to be shelved as a book and too stout to go in a cuttings file. So although definition is difficult there is no difficulty recognizing what, for news library purposes, is a pamphlet.

The range of material is as wide as that of press cuttings and includes press handouts by embassies, industries, and pressure groups, local government departmental reports and minutes, house journals, society handbooks and annual reports, advertisement brochures and simple propaganda. We can conveniently include government publications here also.

Some libraries file slender pamphlets among cuttings and this is certainly convenient in use. It cannot be done on any scale, however, or the pamphlets will obstruct access to the cuttings. Furthermore, there is no check against losing them. Since by definition they are too slender to be shelved with books one sometimes finds them loosely bound between manila folders in subject groups (i.e. all National Trust, all anti-noise literature) and shelved with books. The folders are, however, very apt to get dirty and present an untidy appearance on the shelves.

All in all, it is probably best to allow pamphlets a sequence to themselves. They can be stored on their spines in vertical files, in lateral files, or in pamphlet boxes. A variation of the closed pamphlet box useful for pamphlets is the open box, with no lid and often cut diagonally from halfway down the visible spine upward to the rear top edge. This exposes sufficient of the contents for the pamphlets to be identified and removed without taking down the box. The great disadvantage of this type of box is dust.

Each container needs lavish guiding of sections. The vertical file makes for easy weeding and accessibility and is sufficiently prodigal of space to take in the variety of odd shapes and sizes that is one of the principal difficulties of pamphlet filing. Where space is an important factor, however, pamphlets are perhaps better stored in boxes on shelves from floor to ceiling. Similarly used, lateral files save at least one third of the space taken up by the same amount of material in quarto vertical cabinets. At *The Times*, pamphlets for long-term retention are arranged in pamphlet boxes stored in compact shelving units. The movement of the presses is controlled by electric motors.

Full cataloguing of pamphlets is a luxury few can afford. They can be closely classified by a scheme in use for books and a detailed subject index employed as a key to their whereabouts.

Dewey works well for those prepared to study it or, alternatively, the scheme chosen for directories. The latter will be less satisfactory because it is unlikely to be narrow enough to give easy access to uncatalogued material. As with books, the subject index to pamphlets can, if desired, be incorporated in the cuttings index, distinguishing the type of material by a different coloured card and a clearly identifiable location mark. Provincial libraries may wish to give a separate sequence to local council reports and other publications.

Somewhat ruthless discarding is necessary to keep pamphlet material in bounds, not forgetting to amend index cards to discarded items. As we have seen, *The Times* maintains two sequences, of temporary and semi-permanent items.

Government publications—blue books and white papers, parliamentary papers, and departmental reports—are vital to a collection of current information. Their arrangement and consequently their retrieval, however, present exceptional difficulties. As we pointed out earlier, titles are lengthy and sometimes downright misleading, the parliamentary numbering system is a study in itself, and the subject covered is often very narrow and unusual.

Fortunately, government publications do not vary greatly in size, which makes them relatively easy to store. Only a minority are large enough to be treated as books, so that most can be housed in the same way as pamphlets, but, if there is any quantity of them, in a sequence to themselves.

They can be arranged in a number of ways. The library which has a full or nearly full collection can file parliamentary papers and command papers by their official numbers and use the Monthly List* as a key. Those owning only a selection of H.M.S.O. material may find it better to classify closely and provide a detailed subject index. (Classification is difficult but a really good subject index may overcome this disadvantage.) *The Guardian* library, with a fairly full collection, arranges by issuing

* *Monthly list of Government Publications* (H.M.S.O.).

department. Annual reports such as the Registrar General's statistics and the various Home Office departmental publications are appropriately subdivided under the department. Treaties go under Foreign Office arranged A–Z by foreign country. Many libraries will be required to maintain also a chronological sequence of Bills while they are under consideration, and to keep Acts until incorporation in the annual volumes of the statutes.

United Nations publications merit a sequence to themselves if stocked in any quantity. Like H.M.S.O. reports they may be arranged by issuing authority, such as F.A.O., W.H.O., etc. Isolated copies, insufficient in numbers to make a sequence, can be treated as books or general pamphlets according to format. The subject index or limited cataloguing provides a key to the location.

(iii) BOUND FILES

Bound newspaper volumes are large, very heavy and awkward to use. Each newspaper retains copies of its publications, although some draw the line at binding every slip edition—a score or more are published by some nationals each day. Nevertheless, the space requirements of bound volumes in a newspaper organization grow at an alarming rate. Bound *Daily* and *Sunday Mirrors* (all editions) take up no less than 25 feet of shelving in a year in two monthly volumes (tabloid size). But *The Times*, a broadsheet, needs less space. At the Newspaper library of the British Museum at Colindale in North London, where copies of British newspapers are deposited under the Copyright Act, there were 450,000 volumes in 1958 and new ones are added at the rate of some 5,000 a year. A year's issues of the *New York Times* take up 7 feet of horizontal shelf space. The bound volumes of broadsheet newspapers are not only very thick, they are, of course, the same size as the newspapers themselves, some 1¼ feet by 2 ft overall.

Modern newsprint is a perishable form of paper. Under

strong light it quickly turns yellow. In time it grows brittle, sewn bindings tear away and pages are easily damaged. The trouble began in the second half of the last century when newspapers were growing in circulation and demanding more and more paper. It was discovered that printing paper could be cheaply made from wood pulp and acres of forest in North America and Scandinavia were cut down to supply the world's newspapers with newsprint. Although adequate for the current day's newspaper the wearing qualities of newsprint are very poor. Accordingly, since about 1860 when mechanical wood pulp came into general use, newspaper bound files have deteriorated and the question of long term preservation is becoming urgent. The paper in the bound volumes before that, when quality paper made from rags was still used for newspapers, is almost as fresh and white as the day it was printed.

If newspaper indexes are to be used with any convenience, bound volumes must be easily accessible near the point of usage. In addition, bound volumes must be looked after for the sake of historical record. All too often they are not, and in many newspaper organisations they gather dust in unsuitable basements, to be clumsily retrieved at the peril of their bindings when required in a hurry.

The proper means of storage, flat on cantilevered shelving, has already been referred to in Chapter Two. In considering the best means of storage and the most satisfactory location, two distinct purposes of bound volumes should be distinguished and separately catered for.

First, let us take the files supplied for ready reference in conjunction with an index. Usage of these, particularly the more recent volumes, is heavy and the files will tend to wear out. They must be stored close by the working library in conditions which may not be ideal as regards light or shelving. It is wise, therefore, to have available for frequent consultation a separate file of loose copies of the paper for as long a period as practicable, thus relieving the pressure on the precious bound volumes. Something can be done to save the situation by substituting microfilmed copies, as we shall see in the next chapter.

Preservation for long-term historical record is quite another matter. Some newspapers go to extraordinary lengths, storing in zinc containers in bank vaults and in country houses. *The Times* prints a small Royal edition on rag paper to ensure durability. Experiments have been made with preservative sprays and covering with tissue but these methods are prohibitively expensive. The deterioration of present-day newsprint is a problem not yet overcome.

A decision has to be taken on how many editions to bind and which ones. The copies chosen for binding must be in perfect condition, stored flat and unused for anything else. Sewing should be of thread and not of wire on any account, because wire will quickly pull away from fragile newsprint and excessive humidity will eventually cause rust. Due to the narrow and uneven margins of newspapers, trimming has to be approached with caution. Covers should be of good quality rexine or buckram, with the surface treated with preservative and softening polish at intervals. It will be necessary to supply the binder with a template, or a rubbing from the spine of previous volumes, not only showing the style of title and date, but positioning them accurately on the spine. Nothing is uglier than a shelf of handsomely-bound volumes with a row of title lines straggling up and down like rookies on parade. Thongs attached to the sides of the spine greatly assist removing the heavy bound volumes from the shelves.

It should always be remembered that bound newspaper volumes are in effect primary sources of historical record on many subjects, and some of the editions thus being preserved may very soon become unique. In spite of the efforts of the British Museum Newspaper Library, at present not enough is being done to ensure that historians of the future will be able conveniently to refer to these magnificent sources for the history and attitudes of our times. Any effort made to ensure that they last a little longer and in better condition is worth making.

CHAPTER SEVENTEEN

Microfilm and Photocopying

We have referred to the problems of deteriorating bound files through the universal use of inferior paper like newsprint. A partial solution to the question, providing some easement of the strain of consultation on existing files, is the use of microfilmed copies of newspapers.

Like the back files themselves, microfilmed newspapers have two functions: long term preservation for historical record and daily use for reference. The same positive film should not be used for both purposes.

A microfilm spool of two months issues of one edition of *The Times* takes up the space of two packets of 20 cigarettes. So the saving in space is enormous. As far as anyone knows, the films are permanent and there is no deterioration over a period of years. So at one stroke microfilm appears to solve two of the principal problems of bound files: space and durability.

If microfilm could fully replace bound files, the bound newspapers could be stored in a place of safety where they would be preserved undisturbed. Logically, no binding would any longer be necessary: all long term preservation and reference copies would be on microfilm. Two positives would be required from each negative (quite a cheap process): one for historical record, one for regular reference use. The negative would be stored in a bank safe perhaps, available when any additional copies were required.

At the present time, however, microfilm viewing equipment is not sufficiently handy and quick in use entirely to replace bound files and many newspaper libraries find themselves both binding and microfilming: perhaps binding one edition and filming others. So the net saving in space is less than it might at first appear—sometimes, indeed, leading to a demand for more.

Spools of microfilm, each containing a few weeks' issues of the paper, are too clumsy for quick reference. A single page is thrown on the screen at a time so that, while this is adequate when turning up a single entry clearly indexed, it is not suitable for a search of the files or for the examination of a number of items over a period longer than that covered by one spool. The rewinding and insertion of new spools is still a cumbersome process with the latest equipment, although 'clip on' magazines offer improvements.

The microfilming system is simple. The newspaper is photographed (usually by an agency specialising in the job) page by page on 35 mm film by means of a special camera which photographs pages very quickly—about 30 a minute. Back issues are photographed direct from the bound files. Current issues are taken from loose copies, a few weeks supply at a time. One foot of film carries just over eight newspaper pages, or 825 to 850 pages on 100 feet of film. The number of issues on a 100-foot spool varies according to the newspaper's paging, of course, but it may be between 30 and 40 issues, or 5 or 6 weeks of daily papers. After developing and fixing, the film is wound on 100 foot spools and stored in aluminium containers. The containers are packed in cartons, clearly labelled with the title, edition and date, like the spine of a book. The negative of the film is always available, so that any number of extra positives can be made as desired.

Special cabinets are marketed for the storage of microfilm, with steel drawers designed to take the spool cartons standing on edge. A useful desk cabinet is available, of which the microfilm reader may be placed. The British Standard on the storage of microfilm recommends that spools be placed flat so that the film lies on its edge. It is claimed that otherwise the weight of the film in the spool may cause it to rub against another strip pressing on it and specks of dust may cause damage. Most of the equipment manufactured for microfilm storage (such as the desk we have referred to) ignores this point.

Each container should be fairly tightly packed to avoid unnecessary movement and should be as dust free as possible. Lacking a cabinet, open book shelving is satisfactory, provided the shelves can be adjusted closely and are provided with a raised edge of the front on each shelf to prevent accidents.

Reading back the film is done with the aid of a newspaper projector or viewing apparatus with a larger than average screen. The image can be enlarged up to 1¼ times the original printed page. When a spool of film has been inserted and projected on to the screen, on some models a lever allows an easy search of the page and the required item can then be enlarged. Pages are turned by means of a handle at the side of the machine.

An an alternative to microfilm spools, there is much to be said for using microcards for newspapers, whereby each issue is reproduced on a 5 in. × 3 in. card. which can be stored like catalogue cards and quickly inserted in a microcard reader. These are not in use for newspapers in this country, however, and since all the capital is locked up in 100-foot spools, it does not look as if a change can be made for some time. Libraries freshly planning to film back issues should seriously consider the use of microcards.

A large and increasing number of British newspapers are now on microfilm, although only a few, (including *The Times* and *The Guardian*), are on sale to the general public in this form. The microfilming agencies, for competitive reasons, prefer not to issue names, but the *Library Association Record* of August 1960 (pp. 256–8) carried a list of those at that time on film.

Both of the microfilm series on sale go back to the first issue, *The Times* to 1789 and *The Guardian* to 1821. The library which buys *The Times* on microfilm and obtains *The Times Index* (also available on microfilm) covering the whole history of the paper has, in fact, bought a library. Nevertheless, *The Times* Intelligence Dept. has not entirely dispensed with bound files for reference but uses a separate microfilm room where *The Times Index* is shelved with *The Times* on microfilm and a viewer.

Some of the snags of microfilm have been emphasized. An immense boon, often overlooked, is that it is possible to make normal sized prints from 35 mm film. Reader-printers are now on the market operating from microfilm and microcard which will produce actual size prints in a few seconds at the press of a button.

A news library has a continual need of additional copies of its press cuttings. Once spare copies of the newspapers concerned have disappeared (and space prevents them being retained for long) a single cutting becomes a unique document. As we have seen, it is easily lost. Furthermore, heavily-used cuttings, particularly if they are long, soon become damaged, rendering perhaps the last paragraph illegible. In addition, library users would often like to have cuttings to keep—at any rate for periods of some days or weeks. All this adds up to a need for extra copies, which can only be prepared photographically.

For the long-term storage of press cuttings experimental projects have been undertaken at the *Minneapolis Tribune* and the *New York Times* towards preserving subject groups of cuttings on microfilm spools. The use of sheet microfilm has been considered by the *Daily Telegraph* but not yet taken up owing to the high cost and laborious preparation.

Whether or not they take enlarged copies from microfilm negatives, many libraries make use of copying machines to reproduce old cuttings. The press cuttings library of the Labour Party, for example, photographs multi-copies of cuttings for use by Members in the House of Commons, and they don't expect to see the copies again. The loan of originals is therefore out of the question. The *Daily Mirror*, as part of a top-level information service, cuts certain items from the press each day and these are photographed in groups on foolscap sheets for retention by those in receipt of the service.

One of the best processes for use in this way is the xerographic principle, such as the Rank Xerox machine, processing any number of dry and clear copies quickly. In place of films or sensitized papers the Xerox method employs a specially coated metal plate made sensitive to light by applying an electrostatic charge. The plate can be re-used many times. The 914 model is simple to operate and will produce seven same-size copies a minute on ordinary paper. Copies can be written on and all colours, types of ink and pencil can be copied. The machine is usually rented, the charge based on the number of metered copies made, so as to avoid the high capital cost of purchase.

A machine employing the contact reflex principle is cheaper to buy and install but there is usually heavy wastage in 'spoils' before good copies are obtained. This is a hidden expense which may also be time-consuming and frustrating.

A more difficult matter than reproducing loose cuttings is photographing from bound files. A bound file cannot be fed through a machine. A large scale Photostat unit is probably the best apparatus here, although the capital cost is considerable and an expert is required to operate it. The Rank Xerox machine will copy from bound books up to 9 in. × 14 in., but it is not at present suitable for copying from bound newspaper volumes.

The Contoura, a 'light box', is simpler in use and it can be carried to the bound file and pressed against the item to be copied. The same objection of high wastage that we have already noted for reflex contact copying is operative here also.

No machine has as yet satisfactorily overcome the problem of reproducing items in left hand columns of right hand pages of bound files where the curvature of the page receding into the spine of a thick volume (probably with narrow margins) causes distortion of the image and renders a contact process ineffective.

What is required is a workable process for bound newspapers costing something between the expensive Photostat method and the cheap 'light box', which will enable good copies to be produced first time and will overcome the difficulty of deeply incised spines in open bound volumes. The Xerox machine offers a lens with a depth of field which partially overcomes this and the equipment is improving.

These are troubles of the early stages of photographic development, however. It seems likely that as apparatus improves photography will solve many of the problems of news libraries—and indeed of libraries in general. It alleviates storage difficulties, it may allow the printing of index references without the intervention of traditional type setting, and it allows the easy reproduction and availability of unique items.

Looking even further ahead, it is probable that one day news information will be programmed on to a computer, rendering much of the discussion in the foregoing pages as out of date as a town crier's bell, but that is a matter for another book.

Bibliographical Note

This book has no bibliography because there has been little writing on the subject of newspaper libraries. The first two important works were both American. R. W Desmond wrote *Newspaper Reference Methods* in 1933 (University of Minnesota Press). *Newspaper Indexing*, by H. A. Friedman, 1942 (Marquette University Press) is the only indexing manual we have. The Library Association Pamphlet No. 11, *Newspaper Libraries*, by J. Lewis, 1952, was the sole British contribution until now. A small pamphlet of 75 pages appeared in Auckland in 1950 under the title of *The Newspaper Reference Library* (Colenso Press). Articles are published from time to time, chiefly in *Special Libraries*, where in the United States the Newspaper Division of the Special Libraries Association has had influence in bringing newspaper librarians together. These can be referred to with the aid of the annual and quarterly volumes of *Library Literature* (H. W. Wilson). A number of other useful books are referred to in the course of the text.

Index